An Arduous Journey

The Story of Philip Smith

Based on true events
L Gregory Smith

Yaloo Books & Fine Literature | Lampasas, TX
ISBN: 978-0-578-52980-6
Title: *An Arduous Journey*
Author: L. Gregory Smith
Digital distribution | 2019
Paperback Edition | 2019

Dedication

I want to dedicate this book to the following: my wife, Melissa, my daughter, Kristin, my son, Steven and his wife Shannah, Philip Smith, Caroline Smith, Jacob Smith Senior, Elizabeth Smith, Jacob Smith II, and my father, mother, and my three brothers who are all now in Heaven.

I also want to dedicate the book to my sisters-in-law, Setta, Silvia, and Rhonda, and thank them for loving my brothers. I want to recognize Henry Langford and David Lancaster for maintaining the beauty and cleanliness of the Smith Cemetery at School Creek by volunteering and working to maintain the beauty and data for the cemetery.

Lastly, thanks to my friends that supported me, and my wife's sister, Christa, and my son, Steven. With me being a digital immigrant, they saved me with technology and support. I also want to thank Ruthie Martin for looking over the manuscript and helping to edit the final copy. Ruthie is one of my best friends and a colleague as we traveled through the joys of public education.

I especially want to thank my life time friend, Thomas English. He illustrated the cover for my book, and he is a world class artist, and a brother from another mother to me.

Preface

This is a true story of a family's adventure of finding a better life in America. The Schmitt family lived in Hessen-Darmstadt, Germany for many generations. They had a farm on which they worked hard to make a living. The provincial government was autocratic, and overtaxed the citizens. If people did not pay their taxes or if they were late in paying, they could be put in jail and/or lose their land.

Many hard-working people had heard of, or read about, people moving to America in search of land, freedom, and the American Dream. The father of the family was Jacob Schmitt. After doing extensive research on my family history, I was drawn into an amazing story that follows in this book.

I was mesmerized as I was going through the history of these incredible people while I was doing the cemetery research. I was working to obtain an historical marker for The Smith Cemetery at School Creek. I felt obligated to write this book so that many more people could enjoy this amazing story. The people in the story were ordinary folks who were able to do extraordinary things during their journeys.

In their travels, the family had become citizens of Germany, Mexico, The Republic of Texas, the Confederate States of America, the State of Texas, and citizens of the United States of America.

The three people in this history who stood out to me were Jacob's sons, Philip and Jake, and Philip's wife, Caroline. Philip was my great-great grandfather.

I hope that you enjoy this story and that you vicariously live through the strife, adventure, determination, love and glory.

Although this book is based on true history, the book is an historical novel that is based on real events. I have chosen to write in some dialogue, as well as what I imagined would be happening with the people in this story in various situations.

While writing this book I became immersed into the story of these brave and determined folks. Johann Friedrich Ernst(8) was the first German to immigrate to Texas in 1831. Jacob Schmitt brought his family over in 1833. The Schmitt's were some of the first Germans to settle in Texas. I hope you enjoy this extraordinary tale.

Chapter 1
Germany in the 1830s

It is the autumn of 1832 in the peaceful valley of South Central Germany on the Rhine River. The family lived on a generational farm near the town of Hessen-Darmstadt in the area of Frankfurt.

Jacob, the patriarch of the Schmitt family, and his son Philip were at a neighboring farm helping to repair the neighbor's fences. While they were gone, two men approached the Schmitt's door and knocked heavily. Jacob's wife, Elizabeth, opened the door. She had five children that were inside the house.

"Who are you and why are you here?" she asked the men.

"The Governor has raised taxes on every working family in the amount of 5%, and the payment is due once per month."

"Payment for this month will be due in 10 days. If your payment is late, or the debt is unpaid, there will be hardship for your family. You will have to surrender property of our choosing, or serve time in debtor's prison."

Elizabeth was quite shaken and went back into the house.

On the trip back to the Schmitt farm, Philip spotted two men walking on the road. The men appeared to have been walking from their house. He pointed it out to his father. Jacob and Philip went back home, where they rested for a while. After they rested, they went outside to tend the fields and finish up some chores. They came into the house, cleaned up, and the family ate dinner at the big wooden table. After everyone had finished eating, and the table was cleared away, Elizabeth asked Jacob to take a stroll.

On a beautiful fall evening while walking on a path in the woods, Elizabeth gazed at Jacob in a strange manner. "While you were gone today, two tax collectors banged on our door. They were extremely rude," she said.

One of the men said, "The governor has raised the taxes. If we don't have an additional five percent in ten days, your property will be taken or we will put you in debtor's prison!"

Jacob didn't seem to be surprised with what Elizabeth was telling him. Jacob spoke to Elizabeth, "Dear one, I am pretty sure that Philip and I saw the two men on our way home. I'm afraid that it will get much worse. There is talk that the governor wants to gain control of as much land as he can, and is using the tax raise as a manner to do that. I have heard talk from many of my friends from the farms as well as from the men in town," Jacob told his wife.

Elizabeth asked, "What can we do about it husband? We have little as it is, and we survive on what we can get from selling produce and livestock from the farm. It is so hard to feed ourselves, as well as our children and the livestock."

"I have heard that there is free land and a fresh start in America," Jacob said.

"Oh! I don't think that we could leave the farm with the children, it would be a terrible ordeal for our entire family," she responded.

"Let us think more about it and consider it seriously. It seems that it will be bleak if we were to stay here without finding some way to make more money for the taxes," he told her quietly. Elizabeth nodded and agreed, and she realized at that moment that the move could be the answer to their problems, albeit very difficult.

When the parents came back into the home, the children were playing inside and were happy, except for 12 year old Philip, who was the oldest child. Philip was a serious child who seemed to have great awareness and intuition. He was a very intelligent young man. He somehow was able to have a different book in his hands every 2 or 3 days.

His father never asked him where the books came from. He knew that Philip was an honest young man, and must have been borrowing the books from wherever he could find them. He also knew that Philip returned every book he read. He did notice that Philip had a passion for reading, and the books he read were of a variety of subject matter. The boy seemed to have a desire to learn everything he could.

The younger children had gone to bed. "What is wrong," Philip inquired. He sensed that his parents were upset, although they were trying hard to hide it. "There is a problem Philip," his father responded. Jacob knew that his son would not be satisfied with any answer except the truth.

"A couple of the governor's men came to our house today and told us that we would need to pay more taxes," Jacob told his son.

Philip replied, "What are we going to do?"

"We only have a few options and we will talk and pray about what we should do," Jacob stated.

"I would like to help you figure this out, if you will let me," Philip said.

Jacob put his hands firmly on Philip's shoulders, attempting to reassure him, and told him, "We will talk and consider all options. You are welcome to give opinions which could help the family decide on what we should do." Then he thanked Philip and told him, "Go to bed, tomorrow will be another day."

Philip could tell by the tone of his father's voice that together, his family would be fine. It seemed as if his father was excited about the possible adventure. Philip went to bed hoping and praying that answers would come to them all tomorrow, or in the days to come.

As time went by, Jacob and Elizabeth were barely able to pay the taxes, and they had many conversations about what they could do about their situation. One night, Elizabeth again asked Jacob to take a walk after dinner. This time they also invited Philip to walk with them. On their stroll, she said to Jacob, "We can't continue this life. We have sold everything of value to pay the taxes. I think we should go to America. Even though it will be hard, it appears to be our only choice, and it certainly will be an adventure."

"I agree, we will sell our land, and start our journey to America," Jacob replied.

Philip had listened very carefully, and seemed to understand the seriousness of the situation that his family faced. He said, "Father, mother, we are all healthy and I can take care of the younger children, and also help you two with anything you might need. I can drive a wagon and I am pretty strong. I can help you when you need to do heavy lifting. I think we should go to America also." Philip had heard his father talk about America many times. It did seem like this strong family could succeed at starting a new life.

Chapter 2
The Journey Begins

In early August of 1833, the Schmitt family had sold their farm and had packed their wagons with their children and belongings. The family had packed everything they needed and left for France. They had two wagons full of necessities. The family would camp wherever they could, after each brutal day of travel.

After about two weeks, they arrived at the port of Calais, on the coast of France. It had already become a difficult journey, and yet they had really just begun. They only had minor problems on this leg of the journey and found shelter and food along the way.

Elizabeth had been born and raised in England in Birmingham, west of London. The family took the ferry from Calais to England. The family still had their wagons and they went across the English Channel. When the family reached the English shore, they left the ship. The family gathered their possessions and proceeded to Elizabeth's childhood home. They would continue to camp for this leg of the trip also. They finally arrived after a week of travel. When they approached the house, Elizabeth saw her mother and father for the first time since her parents had visited her and her family three years before.

She and the children rushed to hug their grandparents crying tears of joy while Jacob was putting up the horses and wagons. Elizabeth's parents were named Richard and Anne. In a few moments, Jacob ran into the house and also gave them both a big hug.

The Schmitt's were able to rest and eat home cooking after nearly a month long journey. After about a week as guests, Elizabeth told Jacob, "I finally am convinced that we are doing the right thing."

"I feel exactly the same Liz, we are doing the right thing," Jacob replied.

The family loaded the wagons on the sixth day. They said their goodbyes to Elizabeth's parents and headed for Liverpool the next day. Her parents were very generous, and gave them money and supplies to continue on the journey. Richard and Anne knew in their hearts that they would never again see Elizabeth or her family again.

The family arrived in Liverpool after a week of travel. There were places they could stay while waiting to get tickets to America. Jacob went to the shipyard soon after they arrived. He went to buy tickets on a ship going to New York City. When he reached the ticket counter, the ticket master had asked him "What is your destination sir?"

Jacob said with a happy tone, "My family is going to America." He purchased the tickets. The family was able to sell their wagons and other goods to help support themselves for the trip.

The ship they would travel on was a typical ship of the day. The ship was of a class that was known as a "packet ship." These ships typically delivered mail, cargo, and people. Many Europeans immigrated to the United States from the port of Liverpool. (6)

The ship was a sailboat, with 3 main sails and was about 200 ft. long and 40 ft. wide. Steam ships were not going to be regularly used until the late 1840's.(8) The name of the ship was the "*HMS Assurance*." These packet ships were often owned by the person that also served as the captain. The rest of the crew were mostly members of the newly formed

"British Merchant Navy." Many other countries soon after created their own merchant navies based on the British version. The day to depart arrived and the family boarded the ship. Everyone was very excited and a little bit scared. The steward showed them their room.

There were only six cabins available, due to it being primarily a transport ship. The rooms were very small, and the family was very cramped. Considering there were two adults and six children in a room that was around 8 feet by 8 feet. It was a small space in which to stay for a voyage across the Atlantic Ocean.

All the passengers had to use a shared restroom in the hall with one shower, and two toilets. There was very little to do on the ship, so the family mostly would look out at the ocean. Sometimes they would gather in the cabin to play cards or tell stories. The trip was fairly calm for the first week.

After becoming settled in their cabin, they were provided with their food. Each passenger would typically be provided weekly, 5 pounds of oatmeal, 2 ½ pounds of biscuit dough, 1 pound of flour, 2 pounds of rice, ½ pound of sugar, ½ pound of molasses, ant two ounces of tea.(6)

The passengers were obliged to cook the food in one common kitchen at the back. The kitchen was 12 feet by 6 feet, and shared by all the passengers. Often a family would only be able to cook 1 or 2 meals per week. At times when there was bad weather and the ship was lurching, they were unable to cook anything at all, and therefore could not provide a warm meal. (8) The name of the ship made Jacob a little calmer, even though it was simply a name. The ship started to sail. All of the passengers were on the main deck while the sailors were working to get the ship away.

The Captain of the *Assurance* was named Rob Johnson. He was a native of England and was around 50 years old. He had been a sailor since her was 16 years old. He was known as one of the best captains in the Merchant Navy by those who knew him. He, in this case, was not the owner, but had earned the title of "Captain" in the Merchant Navy.

The First Mate was named Kelly O'Rourke, and he was born in Ireland and had served almost 20 years in the Merchant Navy. One of the two was always on the bridge, and usually they both were there together. They were both seasoned sailors with a great deal of experience.

After a week of clear sailing and calm water, Captain Johnson and First Mate O'Rourke were on the bridge on what seemed to be a normal day. Suddenly, O'Rourke, who was looking through a spyglass at the horizon, said in a concerned voice without moving, "Captain, I think we might have some trouble."

Johnson grabbed the spyglass from O'Rourke and took a long look at the horizon ahead. He said to Kelly without moving, "You are right, it looks like it is going to be a very large squall." He ordered O'Rourke to "summon the steward to the bridge."

O'Rourke answered, "Aye captain."

Kelly went below and came back with the steward. Captain Johnson spoke to the steward in a solemn tone, "Steward, I need you to quickly tell all the sailors that we will be encountering a rather strong storm ahead of us. Please take the normal actions for this event. Also, please address all the passengers and tell them what is going to happen, and what they will need to do."

The steward responded, "aye aye, Captain." He then turned and went to do his duties.

After the steward left the bridge, Kelly remained on the bridge and said to Captain Johnson, "Rob, this is going to be a big one."

Rob replied, "Aye, my friend, but we know what to do, and we have survived them all, and we must follow our procedures." All was well on the bridge.

The Schmitt family was in the cabin when there came a loud knocking on the door. The Steward was letting all the passengers know that the captain wanted to notify everyone aboard that the ship was approaching a strong storm. The steward said, "The captain would not be able to steer around it in time."

It was one of those ocean squalls that can build up very quickly, and could get very violent. The steward told Jacob, "The ship is going to encounter a strong squall ahead." You, and your family, will need to stay in your cabin until we get past it. I need for your whole family to stay on the floor and only use the toilet only if there is an emergency."

Jacob asked "When do you think we will face the storm?"

The steward answered, "Very soon, so you and your family should take care of any business they need as soon as possible. You should go quickly because we are approaching the storm soon. Storms out here can last from fifteen minutes to over an hour. You will hear a warning bell, and you must all get into your cabin and hunker down on the floor until you hear the bell again. That will be the 'all clear bell', and it means that the danger is over.

Jacob told his family, "Go to the toilet and try to do your business, even if you don't think you need to. Please hurry and get back to the cabin as soon as you can." Everyone minded Jacob, and they were back within a very few minutes. The problem was that all the other travelers had been told the same thing, so the toilets were crowded. Everyone made it back to their cabins before the warning bell rang.

Once the family all returned to the Schmitt cabin, all the children were scared, except Philip. He was helping his parents calm the younger children down. About 3 minutes later they all heard the warning bell. It was a loud clanking sound. They did what they were told to do, and stayed on the floor holding on to the furniture that was screwed into the floorboard.

Within a couple more minutes the ship shuddered with a violent lurch. The ship was moving to the point that it was going back and forth which caused a 45 degree pitch with each pounding wave. All of the children, other than Philip, were crying and scared. This continued for about 15 minutes, then, suddenly, the ocean was calm. The family all hugged together with joy on the cabin floor just as the "All Clear" bell rang.

The rest of the voyage was fairly calm, and the family spent most of the time outside enjoying the beautiful sky. They were feeling so thankful that they had made it through a remarkable event.(1)

One day when the ship was getting very close to North America, something wonderful occurred. The family was in the cabin except for Philip, who was on the deck. Philip suddenly burst through the cabin door and shouted, "Everyone, you must come with me at once!" Before anyone could reply to him he had left the cabin abruptly and was already running up the steps to the upper deck.

When the family reached the deck, they saw Philip who was waving his hands and motioning for them to come to him. Jacob was heading quickly toward Philip and asking, "What is the matter son?" Philip did not reply but pointed to the water and was bouncing a little. He couldn't stop bouncing.

When the family reached Philip, they realized why he was so excited. Off of the deck around 200 feet away, there, in all their glory, was a pod of whales swimming near the surface. They could see the water coming up from the whales' blowholes. Every so often, one would breach the surface and splash back down into the water. The whole family stood there in awe until the whales disappeared from their sight.

The ship arrived in New York City about three weeks after they started sailing. When they got very close to the city, the family gathered on the bow to see the magnificent view. None of them had ever seen such a grand sight. Jacob had been to Frankfurt once, but it was nothing compared to the sight they were seeing now, New York City. The ship docked and dropped the immigrants off on Ellis Island. The Statue of Liberty would not exist until it was given as a gift from the French people to the United States later. It was dedicated on October 28, 1886.(6)

The children were giddy and squealing, and Jacob and Elizabeth were hugging and full of joy. They left the ship and were taken across the bay in a oar boat to the city. From where they landed, they were brought to a large building on the mainland for their temporary stay. There was housing and food available for the new immigrants.

There were around fifty families in the shelter, which also served as the immigration processing center. The civil servants processed all that passed through there before certifying them to be legal immigrants.

An 1830s British Packet Ship

There were people from many different countries, and during this period, there were a large number of immigrants from Germany. After processing, families would head out in many directions, each one searching for their own "American Dream."

While in the community, there was a colony forming to continue on to Texas. Jacob and Philip joined the group that was assembled. "We are forming a Texas Colony. You will find free land with good farm or ranch land in Texas," the agent stated. There also was talk among the crowd of how wild and dangerous Texas might be.

A delegate of Stephen F. Austin happened to be visiting New York seeking potential settlers in the Texas Territory. He spoke to the immigrants of a beautiful place where they could gain a section of land or more. Jacob sought out Austin's associate with Philip by his side. The delegate's name was Ronald Jeffery. He went by the nickname, "Ron."

Jacob stated to the delegate, "Please tell us more about Texas." Mr. Jeffery told Jacob and Philip that "Texas is a wonderful place. There are mountains, deserts, natural springs, beautiful rivers and lakes, old growth forests, rolling hills, and excellent farm land."

Suddenly, there was a voice that stated, "Ron is exactly right. The countryside is beautiful, and the people are brave and very civilized." Ron, Austin's agent, turned quickly to that familiar voice.

"Well, Stephen F. Austin, as I live and breathe." Standing with some other men, it certainly was Austin in the flesh he realized. Austin said to the Jacob, "Ron is my right hand man, and he didn't realize that I would be here at this time." The men talked for a long spell, and Jacob and Philip were enthralled. The two returned to their room and gleefully told Elizabeth and the children the news.

After many very intense and serious conversations between Jacob, Elizabeth, and Philip, they agreed to join the "Texas Colony." Jacob signed documents with the Texas delegation which would grant said holder of one family, land in the Texas Territory. The contract stated that the new owner must work the land, and not sell any of the land for at least 5 years. If those requirements were met, the owner would have a clear deed forever.

At a meeting on deck of the Texas Colony, Ron told Jacob, "When you arrive and leave the ship in Texas, there will be an agent to meet you and your family. He will guide you to the processing station. He will also assist you with your citizenship. It will be a Mexican citizenship because Matagorda is in a territory belonging to Mexico. There will be a place for your family to stay in Matagorda. The agent will also arrange an appointment with a Mexican official at the court house. It will be there that you will be offered your choice of land."

"After you choose the land, there will be a secretary of the Republic of Mexico who will explain the paperwork. If everything is legal, you and your wife will be the proud owners of one parcel of land where you can settle. Should the land become part of Texas, or the United States of America, the secretary will assist you through those processes as well."

"Mr. Austin is acting as the broker, and he has an ironclad contract with the Republic of Mexico, and the contract will be binding. Best of luck to you and your family, and I know you will be very pleased," Ron related to the colonists.

Chapter 3
Texas Bound

In a few days, Jacob, along with Philip, went to the ticket master in New York. This ticket master asked the same question that was asked in Liverpool, "What is your destination?"

Philip jumped up and yelled "We're going to Texas!" They purchased their tickets and the next day boarded a ship bound for Texas. They were fortunate to have had a peaceful voyage from New York to Texas along the coasts of the Atlantic Ocean and the Gulf of Mexico.

In December, 1833 the family who left their generational homeland in Germany, had made it all the way to Texas. The ship from New York landed on the Matagorda Peninsula about two weeks later. The boat docked and the passengers left the boat. The Texas Colony had arrived at their new homeland. As Jacob Schmitt brought his family off the ship, there was a line for the new immigrants to register as legal immigrants of Mexico.

It soon was Jacob's turn to register at the table. When asked his name, he printed, signed and said "Jacob Smith." He also registered Elizabeth and his children: John, Lewis, Margaret, Emily, Mary Ann, and Philip all by the surname, "Smith." From that day on, none of them would ever speak or sign their last names as Schmitt, but forever forward they would be the Smiths, as they now were Americans.

There was also a shelter where they could stay as long as needed in Matagorda. When registering, each head of each family would arrange an appointment with the magistrate at the courthouse to agree to the parcel of land that they would soon own in the area.

Jacob, with Philip tagging along, went to the courthouse on the designated date and time. Jacob was shown maps with available sites from which he could choose.

He had met with Stephen F. Austin in New York when he was there. Mr. Austin signed a letter for Jacob to allow him and his family to receive a league of land when he reached Texas. Jacob studied all of the available land, and there was a league of land available just inland from the Gulf of Mexico on the Matagorda Peninsula. He agreed to own the parcel if he would work the land and not sell any part of it within 5 years. A league is 4428.4 acres or three square miles.(6)

A small town had appeared at the port. There were several vendors due to the many immigrants who came off of ships that landed at this port on Texas soil. Jacob advised Elizabeth, "Dear, please find a comfortable spot to keep the little ones. Philip and I are going to get a wagon and some oxen so that we can head to our new home."

The two wandered through the organized chaos until they found what they were looking for. Jacob purchased a sturdy wagon and found two healthy oxen, which he also bought. He and Philip drove the team back to the landing. The family gathered and loaded all their belongings and they started off to their future home.

Jacob had gotten directions to his new ranch. It would be about a two hour drive to their new place. The time flew by and the family enjoyed the scenery on the trip. Jacob stopped the wagon and paused. He said to his cherished family, "If you look ahead near that bunch of trees, you will be seeing our future home."

He and his family rode past the stakes that had flags on the top. They were finally home. They planned to build a big house at a later time. Jacob, Elizabeth and the six children were home on their new land. The Smiths lived in tents for awhile as they got settled. In a few days, they saw several wagons heading to the family's ranch. When the first wagon reached the tent, a middle aged man told Jacob, "Howdy, I am Ben Booker. A few of us neighbors would like to help you build your first house here in Texas."

"Well kind sir, we thank you with all our hearts," Jacob replied.

With all the men working together they finished the small house. The house was primitive, yet it provided them shelter. Within the next few days, Jacob and the boys, along with some neighbors, dug a well near the cabin. In the meantime, there was a year round creek where they could get fresh water.

The ground water had been found by a local water witcher, using his divining rod. He found the water fairly quickly, and it seemed to be a strong source of water and very shallow. They secured the inside of the well with flat rocks that they drove into the vertical soil. They also drove rocks into the bottom of the well.

They then they made a round, wooden cover that had a circular hole that was slightly larger than the water bucket. Next, they erected two poles to support a pulley. There was a round, cured tree trunk about 4 inches in diameter. They had carved semi round downward cuts where the log would fit in the top of both poles.

They then measured the depth of the bottom of the well and cut a strong rope that would reach the bottom. They wound the rope around the tree and attached a round handle with a grip and a bucket attached to the bottom of the rope. The grip control for the rope was attached to the horizontal log. They would leave the bucket upside down on the platform they had built when they did not need to procure water from the well.

When they needed water, they would grab the bucket with the rope attached to the handle, placed it through the hole and lowered the bucket down below the water level. They would then turn the simple pulley to draw the water up.

The neighbors would come back each day to help Jacob and the boys construct corrals and a barn, to take care of the livestock that they would soon acquire. It was traditional for neighbors to help when new families moved in. When the barn and corrals were completed, they began working on the big house. It took hard work, and several weeks, before everything that was necessary was completed.

When the house was finally built, the Smith family invited all of their neighbors to a celebration. Each family would bring food, and Elizabeth and the girls cooked. It was a grand old time for the Smiths and their neighbors. That night when the family retired, Elizabeth snuggled up to Jacob and said "Husband, we did it, we actually did it. I love you." Jacob leaned over and gave her a loving kiss.

They worked slowly but steadily. Jacob had dug another well near the big house with his sons and some friends. This well was very similar to the first one. Jacob had hired a few ranch hands. He had a small amount to pay them and he signed contracts which said that each cowboy would earn one head of cattle for each three months of work. They also would have free food and shelter.

He asked two of his cowboys to ride to neighboring ranchers in case the cowboys found some worthwhile cattle. The cowboys were happy to go, and could drive the cattle home if some were purchased during their trip. They ended up at a nearby ranch, which had a sign that said "Chickens and cattle for sale." It seemed exactly where they needed to be.

When the cowboys returned, Jacob said to Liz and Philip, "This will be the start of the Smith Ranch." The guys bought a rooster and ten fertile chickens. They had brought home the wagon and put the chickens in a makeshift pen. They also bought a sturdy, young Hereford bull, and twelve mixed breed heifers in healthy condition. The ranch hands stopped by the general store and bought seeds for planting and a fifty pound bag of chicken feed. Jacob was going to start his cattle ranch with his first livestock for the ranch.

He also would till the pasture land to sow grain the next spring so that they would have feed for the livestock, and vegetables for his family. He also purchased two horses and another wagon. He kept the oxen and wagon they had gotten when they got off the boat. Because of the generous gift by Elizabeth's parents, Jacob and Liz had enough money to purchase things needed for the ranch.

The land was different than the farm he had in Germany. The climate was much more temperate than their previous farm. Also, the land was sandy and very promising for growing many things. He had always been a farmer, so he had great knowledge and skills about the way of life. Jacob was excited that he was going to be a cattle rancher in Texas.

Texas at that time, 1833, was still a territory of the country of Mexico, and it was known as "Tejas." The new settlers called themselves "Texians," and the Mexicans called them "Tejanos" if they were of Hispanic decent. Others were called "Gringos" if they were from European decent.

Jacob settled on land near the coast, and created his cattle ranch. His experience as a farmer, and the sandy soil would help him have a very successful ranch. "A 'league' of land is a term used in the south, primarily in Texas and some other border states. Due to the prior Spanish ownership, land was typically granted in leagues in Texas. It was a land grant from Mexico, brokered by associates of Stephen F. Austin. (7)

Map by Carlos E. Castenada

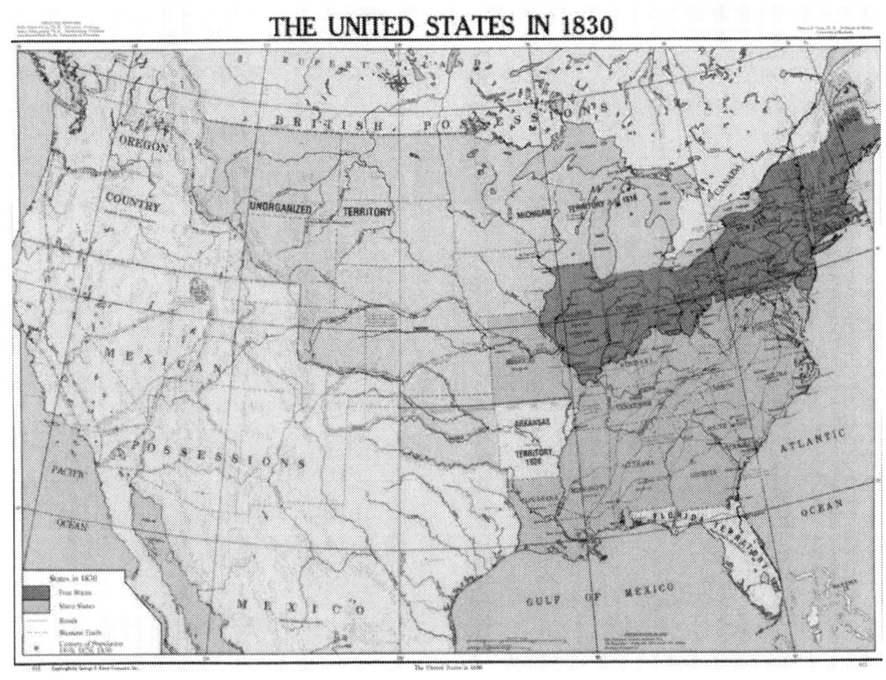

Map of Texas from 1820-1836

By Carlos Casteneda

Chapter 4
The Uprising Has Begun

In 1831, the Mexican authorities delivered a cannon to the town of Gonzales. It was to help fend off the frequent Native Indian raids. In the following couple of years, the Mexican Generals and politicians in Mexico City were becoming nervous about Tejas, and that there was unrest with the settlers.

The authorities judged that there might be trouble, and decided to send troops to Gonzales to retrieve the cannon, in case it might be used against them. Colonel Domingo de Ugartech, Commander of all Mexican troops in Texas, sent 100 dragoons to Gonzales to get the cannon.

The people of Gonzales refused the offer at first. The people then stalled for a few days. In the meantime, folks went to nearby communities to get help. Two days later, the townsfolk gathered and unanimously voted to keep the cannon. The people of Gonzales had made a battle flag which had the image of the cannon on it, and the words "Come and Take It." They had readied themselves for battle with reinforcements coming into town from the surrounding areas.

The small army rode from Gonzales to the Mexican camp and gunfire erupted on both sides. The Mexican army fled in retreat. This became the first military engagement of the Texas Revolution. This was on October 2, 1835. (6)

COME AND TAKE IT

The battle flag of the Gonzalez militia was used in the first military conflict of the Revolutionary War of Texas. The Gonzalez militia carried a hand drawn flag when they battled the Mexican Army on October 2, 1835. (6)

The Texas settlers, or Texians, would declare independence from Mexico on March 2, 1836. (4) Matagorda province was far away from the fighting. The whole family would reside on the ranch during the war, except for Philip.

At this time, Philip had become a very effective wagon driver that began in Germany. Sam Houston was elected to command the Texian army. You may have some knowledge of the massacre at the Alamo. The battle lasted from February 23 to March 6, 1836. General Antonio Lopez de Santa Anna, will be referred to as Santa Anna going forward. (6)

The Alamo is a Spanish mission near San Antonio de Bexar. It is estimated that Santa Anna had more than 1500 soldiers and there was somewhere between 182 to 257 Texians according to eye witnesses. (7). On the early morning of March 6, Santa Anna's army stormed the mission and killed all the defenders. William B. Travis, Davy Crockett, and Jim

Bowie, were among the dead. Travis and Bowie had sent non-combatants to Gonzales to warn the people of what was about to happen. There were an estimated 600 Mexican soldiers killed during the battle. (8)

There were reports that six Texians surrendered, yet Santa Anna had them executed. Travis had messengers ride to meet Sam Houston to ask him for reinforcements, but the massacre occurred before they could get help. There were less than 100 Texian reinforcements that showed up to the Alamo before the final battle. (9)

Houston was gathering up as many men as he could and there were many that had heard about the Alamo. The Texians were livid when they heard about the massacre at the Alamo. Hence, before every battle that was fought, The Texian war cry was "Remember the Alamo!"

Almost all of the able bodied men wanted to join the Texian army. General Houston gathered as many men as he could find to fight. He knew that the men weren't ready for battle. Houston began a retreat to the southeast so that he would have time to train his men.

He also would use it as a military strategy. In the meantime, Santa Anna's troops marched on and also stormed the mission at Goliad. The Mexican army killed all the Texians that were there in a ruthless massacre. All of the souls were taken with no remorse.(9)

Santa Anna and his army had a final goal. "Find Sam Houston, and the Texian Army, and slay all of them as we have done at the Alamo and Goliad. 'We will show no mercy' became the battle mission cry from Santa Anna. With that heartless message to his troops, the Texas Army proceeded southeast in strict military formation. (7)

Chapter 5
Tejas Becoming Texas

Philip Smith of Matagorda had heard of the war and drove his wagon to where Sam Houston's army was mustered. Philip was enraged about the slaughter of Texans at the Alamo and Goliad. He decided to join the army. He was a very stubborn young man, and he knew his mind. He told his father and mother he was going, and they insisted he not do so. He had never disobeyed his parents, but he was going to do so now. Philip was 14 years old at the time.

He left that day for the front of the war. When he reached the battle front, he parked his wagon, and went to the biggest tent he saw. He was stopped by an officer, and the captain asked Philip, "What do you want?"

Philip said, "I want to speak with General Houston."

The captain told him, "Give me your name and let me know what it is that you want to say to him, and I will tell him."

The captain left for Houston's command tent, and told the general what Philip had said. He told Houston, "That boy said he would not leave until he could talk to Sam Houston."

Houston told the captain to "Escort Philip to me, I will talk with him." When Philip arrived, he bowed and shook hands with Sam Houston.

He told the General, "I want to fight with the Texians and defeat Santa Anna and his troops."

Houston paused for a moment, thinking this is something rare. Houston asked Philip, "How old are you young man?"

Philip replied while standing at attention and saluting, and spoke in his deepest voice, "I am 14 years old General Houston." Houston returned the boy's salute.

Houston then told the boy, respectfully, "You are too young to fight, but I have an important assignment for you. It was reported that you are a skillful wagon driver."

Philip responded, "Yes sir, I can drive a stage coach and any kind of wagon." Sam Houston looked hard at Philip and he admired the young man. He paused a moment and stated, "Private Smith, I am enlisting you in the Texas Revolutionary Army as a teamster." Philip Smith was assigned to drive his wagon to the front, and gather up women, children, and wounded soldiers. He then was to drive the wagon to Galveston to keep the innocent out of harm's way. Philip started his enlistment on that day with his first trip to Galveston. (1)

Houston had a place arranged to receive the non-combatants and injured soldiers in Galveston. Houston ordered the Captain to provide Philip with a map and an address. Philip told the Captain that he is familiar with Galveston and he knows where the place is. The Captain said, "Private, you are on duty and are ordered to make your first trip." He then saluted Philip and Philip saluted back. This would be the first time Philip made the trip from the front to transfer the non-combatants and wounded. It also was the first time he had seen or experienced war. It made him vomit. He had never seen or smelled the horrible senses caused by war.

Luckily, he thought, no one saw his reaction to the carnage. He steeled himself and got to his wagon and began helping the passengers get aboard. He made several trips between Galveston and the front, and he had trained himself to be brave, even though he never got used to it.

Houston continued his retreat south-eastwardly, and Santa Anna split his army into three factions. By then, the Texians had developed military skills. Sam Houston was a learned man. He also was well versed on military history.

He had read about the Battle of Waterloo, which ended the Napoleonic Wars. He used a similar strategy that the Duke of Wellington and his Prussian allies used that caused the defeat of Napoleon Bonaparte at Waterloo.(9) On April 21, 1836, Houston had found a perfect place for his "Waterloo" to defeat Santa Anna. (6)

Santa Anna's troops were weary, low on supplies and split up. The main Mexican troops were drawn into an open area surrounded by trees and Texians. The place is near San Jacinto. The Texians routed Santa Anna's army in an 18 minute battle. Houston's army captured more than 600 soldiers, including General Santa Anna himself, dressed as a private. (6)

Santa Anna signed a surrender document stating that Mexican soldiers would retreat back to the Rio Grande. The Texians would own the new territory at that moment. The Texans now owned the territory north of Rio Grande River. The Mexican name for the river was 'El Rio Bravo Del Norte'. The word spread quickly throughout Texas, and there was great joy as the people heard the news. It was the beginning of The Republic of Texas. (7)

There would be many meetings and disagreements while forming the government of a new republic, but it came to be. The Republic was born on March 2, 1836 and annexed by the United States of America on December 9, 1845 when it was admitted to the Union as the 28th state. The transfer of power from The Texas Republic to the State of Texas formally took place on February 19, 1846. (8)

Chronology of the Capitol of Texas

On March 2, 1836, fifty nine delegates gathered on what was called "Washington on the Brazos." The territory would be owned by Mexico until the Texans created a working government. The delegates met in a stagecoach Inn. It was there that the delegates wrote the Texas Declaration of Independence from Mexico.(6) From that day until the present, Texas celebrates March 2nd as Texas Independence Day.

After the signing of the document, they moved the government to various places in 1836. They had a short stay at the Washington on the Brazos. The government then moved to Harrisburg, Galveston, and finally Columbia. The government met for 3 months in Columbia, which later became West Columbia. During that time, the representatives elected Sam Houston as the first President of The Republic of Texas. Houston was elected on October 22, 1836. (6)

At Houston's request, Congress soon voted to move to the unincorporated town of Houston, which was named after the president. The government resided in Houston until Mirabeau B. Lamar was elected the 2nd president of the Republic. Lamar urged the congress to move the government of Texas to Austin, in 1839. The town had previously been named, "Waterloo." Lamar convinced the congressmen to officially rename the town "Austin," in honor of Stephen F. Austin. Lamar wanted to be closer to the expansion of the Republic farther north. (6)

There was quite a bit of movement, and the capitol was moved back to Houston in 1842. The town was not conducive to being the center of government. The town was a "wild west" town at that time. The congress decided that Austin would be the best place for the capitol city and voted as such. The reasoning to locate the capitol in Austin was due to being in a more northern location. It also was a more civilized place than the city of Houston at that time as well. The government was moved to Austin in 1846. (6)

Austin has remained the capitol of Texas from that time until the present. The congress voted to build a capitol building. They decided to build a magnificent building, and they voted as such. It was constructed from 1882 to 1888. Architect, Elijah E. Meyers designed the building in 1881. At the time it was finished, it was designated as the seventh largest building on earth. It was, and still is, larger than the U.S. Capitol building in Washington, the District of Columbia. (6)

The building was constructed with pink granite, which came from a quarry near Marble Falls, Texas. That region is part of the ancient Llano Uplift, which was an intrusion where the magma pierced the crust of the earth over a few hundred square miles in diameter. It took six years to complete, and it was quite magnificent, indeed. (6)

Chapter 6
The Russler Family comes to America

The Russler family lived in England during the 1840s. Caroline Russler received a letter from her aunt, Alicia, who lived with her husband William in Ohio. Caroline opened the letter and read it with great enthusiasm. Her aunt described their immigration to America about a year ago. They settled in Ohio and she stated in her letter what a wonderful country the U.S.A. was to live in. They were very happy and urged the Russlers to consider also immigrating to America.

Caroline shared the letter with her family, and they all thought that it was a wonderful idea. They began planning their journey to Ohio, U.S.A. Around a month later, the Russler family, including her father, Robert, her mother, Susan, and her brother, John as well as herself, were set on going to America. They would take the trip to New York, and then find their way to Ohio and her aunt's home. They lived in Ohio for awhile.

While there, the family worked when they could. After a few months and were told that there was free land in Texas. They were also told that as long as you work the land, a family could own the land outright after a certain period of time. The family decided to travel to Galveston, which was a burgeoning village on the Gulf Coast in Texas.

They traveled back to New York by train with their possessions. While in New York, they then booked transportation by ship to Galveston. The family left the port of New York within two days. The voyage was calm and pleasant. The Russlers were enjoying their trip and getting excited about landing in Texas.

Suddenly, there was a terrible, loud sound and the ship suddenly stopped. Everyone standing on the main deck were suddenly thrown off their feet and landed a few feet from where they were standing. John shouted, "What happened?"

The deck mate heard him and hurried over towards the passengers and told them, "The ship has hit some rocks below the surface. There is no major damage, but the ship will be disabled from sailing until some repairs are made."

The ship was not badly damaged, but it was unable to sail. Although no one was seriously hurt in the accident, and the baggage was secure, everyone in the boat was extremely upset. The captain and crew were very helpful and kept the passengers calm. Two days later, another ship passing by turned and checked on the wrecked ship.

The relief boat transferred all the passengers and crew with their life boats. The captain assured the passengers that as soon as they made landfall, he would arrange a small cargo ship to immediately return to the wreck and salvage all the gear and luggage. The passengers would be able to retrieve their baggage at the Galveston Hotel within a couple of days.

When the Russlers landed they found a hotel where they could stay for an extended amount of time at a low cost. It was the Galveston Hotel. Their plan was that they could make arrangements to meet with Stephen F. Austin's delegate to get their own land while they were in Galveston. It was during this period that Caroline met Philip.

Chapter 7
Philip's Greatest Adventure, Romance

After the war ended, Philip returned to the family's ranch near Matagorda. Philip had lived and worked with his father on the ranch. He got a job as a stage coach driver. His usual route was from Matagorda to Galveston and then back to Matagorda after a rest of a day or two.

He would generally stay at the Hotel Galveston when he was in town. After one trip from Matagorda to Galveston, he was in the lobby of the hotel and he saw what he thought was the most beautiful lady he had ever seen.

Philip was usually a very social being who never met a stranger. But in this moment, his heart was thumping and he felt his face turn red. He couldn't believe himself that he was too shy to approach the lovely lady. He seemed to be frozen with anxiety, and did not introduce himself.

On the return trip to Matagorda, up on the stage driver's seat he could not stop thinking of the lady and that he (of all people) could not get the nerve to introduce himself. After all, he had been to war. He made it back to the ranch and could not stop thinking of her.

When he was home, nothing had changed. His mother knew that something was bothering him, women's intuition most probably. She found a private moment with him and said "Sir Philip, what is so heavy on your mind?"

Philip was nervous about talking to her, but she was his mom and she had always been there for him. He replied, with a stutter, "Mother, I saw the most beautiful girl I have ever seen in my life in Galveston. I just couldn't get the nerve to introduce myself. I was thinking, is she married, does she think I'm ugly or hideous?"

With the wisdom of a mother, she replied "Philip, you are a smart, wonderful, and handsome man. Any girl would be proud to know you. If you see her again, you must introduce yourself. Life is short, and there are moments in life, that you need to seize. This seems to be one of those moments that you need to act on."

1850's Stage Coach

Chapter 8
Can't Get Her Out of My Mind

Philip had returned to the ranch in Matagorda, and had a lay off for a week until his next stage coach trip to Galveston. He would help on the ranch with the work, but his mind was consumed with that beautiful lady. He chastised himself over and over mentally that he had not acted on his desire to meet her. He told himself, if I ever get the chance again to meet her, I will be determined to follow through. He also thought many times that there is a good chance that he might never see her again. He didn't know her name or anything about her.

He tried to keep his mind on other notions besides that vision of a lady, who he can't seem to get out of his head. The seven days before he drove the coach back to Galveston seemed like an eternity. His mind seemed to run like one of those steam engine trains on a fast track. Oh well, if I have a chance to meet her, I will definitely act on it. I hope that I do not make a fool of myself.

Philip had very little formal education. His parents sent him to the small, public school in Darmstadt for Kindergarten through 5th grade. They would have to pay tuition for him to attend the higher grades, and they couldn't afford it. Philip was an intelligent child and he learned quickly.

By the time he was in the 5th grade, he had already become an avid reader. While his mother would do as much home schooling as she could, there just was not enough time. She was not a highly educated lady, although she was a wonderful wife and mother. She also was a skillful farmer.

Philip said to himself, "This is the first time that I have become totally unsure of myself. I wonder what she might think of should we ever meet. I hope she will like me."

Chapter 9
The Story of Lightning

Lightning was born a race horse. He had raced as a yearling and a two year old. On the first race of his three year old season, he had a collision with another horse during the race, in the final turn. Lightning and the other horse got tripped up, and the two horses went down together in a heap. It looked pretty bad.

The tenders went on to the track to see if Lightning could stand up. He was able to get up and walked gently back to his racetrack stable. A veterinarian, Dr. Scott Rushing, came by to examine Lightning. The horse's owner, Joe L. Anderson, was in attendance, as well as his jockey, William Walter, whowas called "Skipper." Very few people knew Skip's real name.

The horse doctor was experienced, and he gave the horse a very thorough evaluation. Skipper said aloud, to no one especially, "That is the grandest horse I have ever ridden. He has the heart of a champion. I do hope that Lightning is well, because this horse is an extraordinary animal"

After a few minutes, Dr. Rushing looked at the owner and said, "Gentlemen, this is a beautiful horse. I have some good news and bad news. The bad news is that he has most probably torn, or seriously strained a ligament near his left front hoof. The good news is that we will not have to put him down. He will regain his health, and have full use of his hoof, but he will never be able to win a race."

The owner, Joe, asked the doctor, "Will he need surgery for the injury?"

Dr. Rushing responded, "We will give him some time, and the ligament may heal up naturally. I will come to your ranch in about two weeks to see how it's going, if that's all right with you."

Mr. Anderson told him, "That will be just fine. If he heals up well enough, what do you think he will still be able to do?"

Dr. Rushing told the man, "If it was me, I would put him out to pasture and breed. He is an excellent horse. He will still be able to run and even pull a wagon eventually, if it's just a serious strain that heals."

Mr. Anderson took Lightning home and let him loose in the pasture. He also loved horses, and he would be crushed if one of his horses had to be put down. Doctor Rushing came by the ranch in two weeks and examined the horse again. He told Mr. Anderson, "This horse is going to be fine. As I said before, however, he has been damaged, and although he could race, the reality is that he will not be able to compete at the elite level."

Mr. Anderson let Lightning be a breed stallion for about a year. He helped make foals, some of which would become champions. A few weeks later, Mr. Anderson was approached by a stage coach company owner named Wade Wooten. He asked if Joe might consider selling the horse to him. When told the amount, Joe decided that it would be a good deal for everyone, including Lightning.

The horse was born to run, and he thought that Lightning would enjoy pulling a coach. The new owner decided to make him a gelding, since he had become a work horse. That is the story of how Lightning went from being a racehorse to a horse that would be pulling a stage coach.

Whether it was luck or fate, Mr. Wooten had designated Lightning to be one of the team that worked Philip's stage route. Philip had fallen in love with the gelding, and was pleased each time that Lightning was on his team. Often times, when he was in Galveston, and had some spare time, he would go to the stable and check him out for a ride.

Philip had asked the stable keeper, Bobby Starr, to ask Mr. Wooten if he could ride Lightning when he was in town. Mr. Wooten was a kind, generous man who also loved horses. Bobby had asked Mr. Wooten if he could check the horse out for Philip to ride, as long as there was enough time before the next route so that Lightning wouldn't be too tired to pull the coach.

Philip would never forget the first time he was able to ride Lightning. It was during a stay for the return trip to Matagorda. He had three days before they had to return, and he was going stir crazy. He decided to have a ride with Lightning. He left the hotel and walked to the stable.

It was early morning and he asked Bobby if he could check out Lightning for a ride. Bobby, the keeper, told Philip, "The boss asked me to tell you that it's fine if you take Lightning for a ride any time you want to within the time guidelines."

Philip said, "Thanks Bobby, are you still playing your guitar?" Bobby replied, "As much as I can."

Philip went in and put a halter on the horse, then brushed Lightning down well, then put the blanket and saddle on him. Next he took off the halter, and gently put the bit in his mouth for the reins. Lightning trusted Philip completely and was very cooperative and calm.

Philip walked him outside, and mounted Lightning. Philip was an experienced rider and everything went well. Philip gave the horse a light kick on his flank and the horse and man proceeded with a walking gait. After a few hundred feet he said, "Let's go," and relaxed the reins and the horse started a canter.

Philip could tell that the horse wanted to run, so he yelled, "Gitty up boy," and completely loosened the reins. Philip gave the horse a light boot to the flank. This urged Lightning and soon there were going at a full gallop. Philip laid his head against the horse's neck and gave him full rein.

They were running like a race horse down a dirt road towards some woods that were ahead. Philip was grinning, and if you could see Lightning at that time, you would swear that he was grinning also. The two were bound as one, as they ran as fast as they could.

When they got to the edge of the woods, Philip pulled on the reins slightly and Lightning gradually slowed down to a walk. Both beings were very happy. Philip guided the horse to an open space in the woods by a running creek.

He took the saddle, blanket and reins off of Lightning, and let him wander down to the creek for a drink of water. Philip had brought a handkerchief in his saddle bags with snacks and a canteen of water for himself. He had also brought a couple of carrots for Lightning.

The boys really enjoyed the ride, and Philip realized in a flash that this was exactly what he and Lightning both needed. His brain had been spinning, and this ride with his favorite horse had suddenly made him become very calm and controlled.

While the two were there, they saw a cottontail rabbit, a small cluster of whitetail deer, and an armadillo. Philip spotted several species of birds that included a large blue heron in the creek, and a red tailed hawk soaring over their heads in a magnificent big sky. He also saw 12 buzzards circling about a half a mile from him, which is a common sight. The actual common name for the birds is Turkey Vultures. Texans just call them buzzards.

Philip let Lightning drink from the creek and he stretched out on the grass and almost fell asleep. What a great day, he thought. After brushing him, Philip got Lightning saddled and bridled, mounted the horse, and started back together to the stable.

Lightning

Note-Worthy Coincidence

Philip's given name by his parents was the perfect name for him, and he probably never knew it. The modern name, "Philip or Phillip" comes from the Greek words, "Pilliopos," which is a combination of "philos" (for love) and "hippos"(for horses), which translates:

" Love of Horses "
That, he surely did.(12)

Chapter 10
Finding Peace

Well, the day finally arrived. He had his brother, Jacob Jr., drive him in their wagon to the stage coach depot. His excitement was beyond belief. Through coincidence or fate, one of the horses on his team was Lightning. He thought to himself, I must concentrate of my driving and the passengers' welfare and safety. He readied the coach, the horses, the baggage, and helped the folks into the coach.

The passengers included a man in a suit, with a lady that was probably his wife similarly dressed who appeared to be in their 50s. There also was a young man that looked as if he might be a cowboy, and a middle aged lady who was traveling alone. They started off for Galveston early in the morning.

The trip was nondescript, with no problems and a smooth ride. They arrived in Galveston around 4:00 P.M. at the stage coach station. Philip helped the passengers down, then brought the luggage to the station, checked in with the depot master, then stabled the coach and the horses. His next trip will be in 3 days the master informed him.

Now, Philip was really starting to think about the ways things might go. He walked to the hotel with his suitcase and stopped off at a flower shop on the way. He purchased a small, yet, beautiful bouquet a flowers of red, white and blue. He was almost skipping as he continued down the street to his hotel. His thoughts were swirling in his brain.

He really couldn't belief that this was happening. Am I deluding myself, am I crazy, is it a gift from God, will she like me, will she hate me?"   He just decided to be himself and hope for her to be the woman he thinks he knows. "Be brave Philip," he said out loud, "You are a good man, and she is my dream wife." He still didn't know if he would ever see her again. He said a silent prayer and continued to the hotel.

Chapter 11
The Courtship Begins

Philip registered at the hotel and went to his room. He had no idea if the 'Girl of His Dreams' would be there, or even be in Galveston, or even in Texas. He shaved, took a bath, and put on the fanciest clothes he had. Dinner would be starting in about 15 minutes in the restaurant. Philip was 28 years old at this time, and had really never had many opportunities to meet ladies of his own age on the ranch.

Philip was a realist, and he knew that the lady who sparked a part of his heart might not even be there. He wondered if he would be brave enough to meet her. He hoped she would be there. He was all cleaned up and neatly dressed. "We will see what happens", he said to himself.

Philip kneeled at the foot of his bed, closed his eyes, and prayed out loud, "Dear Lord, if this is to happen, it is because of you. I sure would appreciate it if I'm supposed to meet the woman of my dreams tonight. I will be forever grateful to you, Amen."

He then stood up, looked in the mirror, and straightened his tie and carefully put on his hat. He picked up the bouquet he had bought from the flower shop earlier in the day and picked up the flowers from the table and went downstairs for dinner.

Philip went down the stairs with his hat in one hand and the flowers behind his back in the other hand. When he reached the bottom he looked around the dining area and Bam! Across the room was the lady he had been waiting for all his life. She was there in the same room and his heart was soaring.

Then suddenly, his heart dropped to the floor. There was a young man with her at her table. His thoughts were scrambled as he tried to decide what he should do. The man looked like he was a few years younger than her, but he very well could be her beau or her husband.

He remembered his promise to his mom and himself, he realized he must meet her, regardless. If she was married or engaged, he would politely introduce himself and quietly walk away. He held the flowers behind his back as he approached their table.

With a big gulp and a deep breath, Philip approached the table where they were sitting. With every bit of courage he could muster, he said politely, "Excuse me for interrupting your dinner ma'am, but I would like to introduce myself to you and your companion."

"My name is Philip Smith, and I live in Matagorda. I drive a stage coach on a route between there and Galveston. I stay at this hotel when I'm in town and had noticed you on my last trip here. You looked so lovely and sweet that I was quite intrigued. I did notice that you were alone last time, and I certainly wouldn't want to bother you. And as you can tell, I seem to talk too fast, and too much, when I get nervous."

The lady, with great charm, grace and a beautiful smile, said to him, "It's very nice to meet you, Philip Smith from Matagorda. My name is Caroline Russler and this is my little brother, John." Philip's heart could begin to beat again. He shook her brother's hand and said, "I'm very pleased to meet you John." Philip took a chance and presented the flowers and gently handed them to Caroline. He sheepishly said, "Beautiful flowers for a beautiful lady."

Caroline accepted the flowers and told Philip, "These flowers are very pretty, thank you kind gentleman."

Caroline asked Philip to "Please sit with us for dinner and we will find out all about you." He politely sat at the table with Caroline and John. The conversation was very basic as they ate dinner. Philip asked Caroline, "Are you a native of Galveston, or a traveler as so many of us are?"

Caroline replied, "My family is from Ohio, have you heard of it?"

Philip replied, "I am embarrassed to say that although I know it is a place in the United States, I do not really know exactly where it is."

Caroline told him that she and her family had traveled to Texas from Ohio to obtain land from the Stephen F. Austin Company. The family took the train to New York City. From there, they took a boat from New York to Galveston. "We are staying in Galveston temporarily because the Austin family's broker is supposed to be here sometime soon.

We are waiting for him to arrive and talk to someone who can explain the process of becoming settlers in Texas. By the way, Ohio is a state which is situated up north. It is bordered by Lake Erie, Pennsylvania, West Virginia, Kentucky, Indiana, and Michigan." (6)

"Although it is a lovely place, our family decided that we can attain our own land by moving to Texas." Philip was impressed with Caroline Russler.

Philip said, "Well you can probably tell by my accent that I'm not a native Texan." Philip still had a fairly strong German accent.

Caroline replied, "Oh I thought you might be from France." Caroline was light hearted and liked to joke about common things.

Philip replied, "My family and I have made a very long journey to get here to become Americans. We have come from south central Germany and my father, Jacob, obtained a land grant near Matagorda. We have been living there for about 12 years. Our family has made a successful cattle ranch. I just had my twenty eighth birthday two weeks ago."

"I will not ask your age, since a gentleman does not do that. I will find out in some way sometime in the future, but with all honesty, it does not matter to me. You actually look like you are a teenager," He said with his strong German accent and a twinkle in his eye. Caroline was actually twenty nine.

John was very quiet and in fact, there was very little conversation at the table, although the ambiance was quite comfortable. The dinner was coming to an end and Philip seized his moment. He asked Caroline, "Would it be crass if I were to ask you to go out to dinner with me tomorrow night? There is a wonderful steak house right down the street and I would really like to take you out for a date. Perhaps John would be welcome if your parents insist on having a chaperone."

Caroline said, "I am not a girl, my parents will not require a chaperone, and I would be honored to go on a date with you tomorrow night."

Philip replied, I am looking forward to seeing you tomorrow around dinner time, and I too am honored." He shook hands with John, and when she held her hand out, he gently held the hand and sweetly kissed the back of her hand.

He went to his room, and he seemed to be floating on air. He couldn't believe that this was happening. He had met the woman of his dreams and it seemed like she was interested in him. He tried to go to sleep early, but his brain could not stop working. What if this was the real deal? What if it wasn't? He fell asleep for a short time, then he woke up thinking of all the possibilities of his future. He had a fitful night, and got out of bed before dawn.

He thought, it would be almost 10 hours before his date with Caroline. What am I going to do to pass the time before we have our first date? He knew he couldn't just stay in his room, he would go crazy and perhaps his brain just might explode. Philip, being a good thinker and the kind of person that couldn't stay still for a long, decided on a plan. He would go to the stables and get his favorite horse and go for a ride.

He got to the stable, greeted Bobby, and signed out his favorite horse, Lightning. He stashed away an apple in the saddlebags that he had picked up in the grocery store on the way to the stable. He brushed Lightning, and put on his blanket and saddle. He gently put the bit in his mouth. They both were ready to go.

Since the stage wouldn't have to leave for two more days, it would not bother the horse to have a ride. Philip had ridden him a few times and although he was working as a coach horse, he liked to run and have fun. It seemed like Lightning knew what was happening, and he whinnied, threw his head around, reared up and did a little dance with his front legs.

Philip packed a small lunch for himself and he had already packed the apple for Lightning. He hopped on the saddle, and rode out of town. Philip decided to go to his favorite spot in the woods and have a picnic. He and Lightning had traveled for a few miles, and they came upon the spot in the woods that they had visited before. He and his horse went into the woods and found an open space next to a spring.

He unsaddled Lightning, took his reins off and let him loose. The horse went straight to the spring, and drank copious amounts of water.

Philip tied him to a nearby tree and sat down to eat his lunch. This time, he had thought to bring some food for Lightning and himself. They had a picnic together. While in the woods on this trip, they saw a variety of birds and animals. Both Philip and Lightning enjoyed their picnic and were both in good mind, and truly relaxed.

Philip brushed and saddled the horse, and gently put the reins back on Lightning. He mounted the horse, and they proceeded through the woods to the other side. Galveston, being a coastal town does not have many wooded areas, so this outing was very pleasant, for both man and horse. They went through the woods and stopped at the spring again.

Lightning and Philip both drank from the natural spring, and he told himself that he would bring Caroline here for a picnic sometime soon. Lightning had been a race horse as a young horse. From the time he was a yearling to becoming a 3 year old, he had raced.

He had won a few races, but because of his injury, the owner had an offer for him to become a coach horse. That is how the two met each other. The two of them started on their way back home. When they were close to town, and the road was smooth, both Philip and Lightning felt like they would like a little fun. The two had developed a strong bond.

Philip broke Lightning into a canter and then into a full gallop for about a half mile while laying his head down on the horse's neck, with their heads together. Philip slowed lightning to a walk, and went back to town, and into the stables. Philip took off the horse's saddle, blanket and reins. He brushed him down in his stall, and gave him some food and water. They both had enjoyed the run, you could just tell.

As Philip was about to walk out of the stable and back to the hotel, he saw Bobby Starr again. This time, Bobby had his guitar on a table. Philip asked him, "Could you sing me a song?"

Bobby jumped up and grabbed his guitar. He said, "I wrote a new song, do you want to hear it? It's about a beetle that I saw this morning. It was huge and shiny green." He sang and played the song and when he finished, Philip clapped his hands together energetically for the musician/stable keeper. Philip told Bobby, "That was quite good, I really liked it."

Philip walked back to his hotel, and he was tired. What a great way to keep his mind from wandering, as well as passing time. When he got back to his room, he took off his boots and fell on the bed. He was asleep in about a minute.

He woke suddenly and popped up out of bed. He looked at the clock in the room. Whew, he thought, I haven't overslept. I won't be late for my first date with Caroline.

He was to pick up Caroline in the hotel lobby at 6:00 P.M. It was 4:30 now. He had plenty of time to get ready and still drop by the flower shop on his way to dinner. Again, he had a bath, shaved, and put on his going to church clothes. He again checked himself in the mirror and decided that it was about as good as it could be.

On the way to the hotel, he stopped in the flower store. This time, he asked the merchant, Denise, that he might need her help. Philip told her, "I loved those flowers last time, but this is our first real date and I would like something special." Denise's eyes got a little larger and a smile appeared on her face. "We have a wonderful bouquet available today. It is yellow roses. They are the unofficial flower of the state, and are beautiful with an incredible scent."

Philip said, "That sounds perfect, I'll take a dozen, and this time in a vase."

Denise told him, "You can't go wrong. Any Texas lady would be thrilled to be presented with yellow roses." Philip completed his purchase, thanked Ms. Denise, and walked toward the hotel.

Philip entered the hotel and there in the waiting room, was his beloved Caroline, her brother John, and an older couple sitting in some comfortable chairs. Philip approached the folks, and they all stood up to greet him. Caroline walked toward him. She looked beautiful. Philip gave her the yellow roses in the vase. Caroline said to Philip, "Good evening Philip those are beautiful flowers. You have met John, but I would like for you to meet my parents, Robert and Susan."

The children were both born in Manchester, England. Philip walked forward and shook Robert's hand and said "It is my honor to meet you sir," then he kissed Susan's outstretched hand, and told her "It is a genuine pleasure to meet you ma'am."

Robert told Philip, "It is my honor to meet you sir. Our Caroline has spoken very well about you."

Susan spoke to Philip and said, "I agree with Robert, it is truly an honor to meet you."

They sat and drank some coffee and had a chat. Then, Susan said to Philip and Caroline, "Now you two have somewhere to go, and we won't keep you." With that, Philip rose, held Caroline's hand and helped her up. As they were turning to walk out of the hotel, Philip told the parents "It is my pleasure indeed to meet the family of dear Caroline. I hope to have many more conversations in the future." With that, the two walked out of the hotel on their way to their first date.

The couple left the hotel and walked down the street to the Steak House. The walk was about 8 blocks. They entered the establishment and were greeted by the host. The sign stated, "We only serve Texas beef, and our steaks are the best tasting in the world." Philip and Caroline were seated and studied the menu. Philip asked her "What looks good to you?"

She said, "The sirloin for two sounds pretty good."

"Sirloin it is, then," Philip stated. He called the server over to their table. The server's name was Josie and she a joyful glow and a lovely smile. In a sweet voice, she asked the couple what their choice was. Philip ordered the sirloin for two, with all the fixings. Josie said, "You will enjoy this and I will be back soon. In the meantime would you folks like something to drink?"

Philip replied, "We would like two glasses of water and a bottle of red wine with two glasses."

Josie winked and said, "I will bring the wine straight away," as she turned and walked to the bar.

During the meal, Philip asked Caroline "Tell me all about you and your family." Caroline told him that "My family was a working family. My parents had gotten the urge to aim for the American Dream .They yearned to have land of their own. They had always lived in a small, single family home in the city and the lure of having their own land was overwhelming."

"The family was contacted by my aunt, Alicia, who with her husband, had immigrated to America and settled in Ohio. Alicia had written us a letter telling us that "there was room in their home if our family came over." Alicia said that "Your family can stay with us as long as you need to."

"I shared the letter with my family, and they all thought that it was a wonderful idea. After some conversation the family had consensus that everyone wanted to move on."

'A few weeks later, we had settled all our business. The Russler family began our journey to Ohio, U.S.A. The Russlers were on their own way to the American Dream. We took the trip to New York, and then found our way to Ohio, and my aunt's home. While there, the family worked when they could and after a while were told that there was free land in Texas, as long as you would work the land."

"The family decided to travel to Galveston, which was a burgeoning village on the Gulf Coast of Texas. We traveled by train from Ohio to New York City. From there, the family went by ship to Galveston where we could make arrangements to get our own land."

Josie returned with a fine bottle of wine and two wine glasses along with the water. She graciously poured the two glasses and said, "The steak will be ready shortly. You two just have a great time."

With both people relaxing, their moods were mellow and they were very happy to be together. Philip had shifted his chair closer to Caroline and said, "A toast for a wonderful night!" They tapped their glasses together and both said, "Cheers" as the glasses touched. A moment later, Josie was serving the most wonderfully smelling beef that they had ever smelled.

Josie encouraged them saying, "Enjoy your meal and I am so glad to meet two such charming people. I have a feeling that this will go very well." Josie left and the couple leaned toward each other and they were looking deeply into each other's eyes. Love was in the air as the two enjoyed their first kiss.

Chapter 12
'Till Death Do Us Part'

Philip and Caroline had already fallen in love with each other. It seems as if it started as 'love at first sight'. When Philip saw her for the first time in the lobby of the hotel, he knew she was the one. The two were indeed in love. After what seemed to be a decade, Philip popped the question to his beloved at another dinner at the steak house where they had their first date.

After the dinner was finished, Philip sheepishly stood up, walked around the table, got down on one knee and said, "Caroline, I fell in love with you the first time I saw you. You appeared to be an angel, floating through the room. I was so awestruck that I didn't have the courage to introduce myself to you."

"You disappeared so suddenly, that I was left on those stairs like a newborn child. I didn't know if I would ever see you again before I had to leave the next morning for the stage coach trip back to Matagorda. I worried and fretted and my mind and heart couldn't stop racing for what seemed to be an eternity."

Philip stood up and went to the side where Caroline was sitting. He got down on one knee and said to her, "I was so fearful that I would never again set eyes on the most beautiful lady I had ever seen. Thanks to luck, and the grace of God, I was able to see you again. I had already fallen in love with you, but as I got to know you, the love became forever for me. I hope, beyond hope, that you feel the same way about me. Dear Caroline, will you marry me?" He extended an open ring box and she took the engagement ring and slipped it on her left ring finger.

Caroline said, "You told me when I first met you that when you get nervous, you talk fast and for a long time. You are doing it again, but, my dear Philip, of course I will marry you. I have been wondering for an eternity when you would finally ask me to marry you."

They stood up at the same time, embraced each other and kissed, and held the hug for much longer than anything close to normal. "I love you Caroline Russler," he said.

"And I love you back," Caroline replied. She then stated, "You seem to have something behind your back. Well, what is it?" Philip pulled out a gold ring and slipped it over her left ring finger. It fit perfectly.

Philip shyly said to her in a very low voice, and with slow words, "Your father has given his blessing to me also." As sweet violin music began to play, the two began to dance as one. After a few dances, they were both very happy and indeed, quite giddy.

Caroline told Philip "Let us go tell my parents and John right away, I don't think I can contain my joy."

Philip replied, "Let's go!" He crooked his arm under her arm and they returned to the hotel. Their steps were more like bouncing.

The two lovebirds got to the hotel and Caroline told Philip to wait in the lobby and she would go get her family. In a very short time, the Russlers were coming down the stairs, each with a wide grin on their face. When they got closer to Philip, they all started talking and congratulating him, whereby he couldn't seem to make any sense of what they were saying.

He grabbed his fiancé gently and said, "Well you just couldn't wait to tell your family the good news."

"That's right, I was just too happy not to let the cat out of the bag. My father let me know of his blessing. I just knew it was real", Caroline replied. Her family and Philip had a joyful time that night.

Robert had some news that even Caroline had not heard. He announced to the small gathering, "We went and talked to the representative of Stephen F. Austin's company today, Susan, John, and I. We are now the proud owners of one section of land close to Victoria, Texas."

There were cheers and happiness with everyone. Philip said, "I know Victoria, I had to substitute for a driver who had gotten sick for a stage coach trip. It is not very far from where my family lives. It's not more than 50 miles from there. When do you think you will be moving to your new place?"

Robert said "We haven't even really thought about when." Philip said, "I'm kind of thinking that Caroline and I can get married on the Smith Ranch.

I will be going there tomorrow, since I don't have a trip to take until next week. I know my parents will be so happy, and will offer you a place to stay. We can be married on your way to your new place."

Susan asked, "Shouldn't you talk to your family before inviting strangers to stay with them."

Philip replied, "If I know nothing else, I am absolutely sure that you have an open invitation from my mom and dad. I will be back in two to three days. I can help move if you need help, and you can stay as long as you want at the ranch."

Philip told Caroline, "I have sure been thinking of Lightning. I am considering buying him from Mr. Wooten if he will sell him. Caroline replied, "I think Lightning should be your horse. We will find a way for you to own the horse."

Chapter 13
The Families Meet

The Russlers had acquired the deed to their section near Victoria. Everyone had agreed that Philip and Caroline would be married on the Smith Ranch when the Russlers were moving to their new place. The time came, and the Russlers packed up everything they needed and left Galveston for the last time to go to the wedding in Matagorda.

In the meanwhile, there was joy and expectations growing at the Smith Ranch. All of the family were working together to build a small but nice looking pavilion on the ranch. They were also preparing for the wedding. Elizabeth found the preacher who would perform the ceremony, and the other preparations were completed and well thought out.

The Russler family was to be at the ranch the following Tuesday, and the wedding would be set for the following Saturday evening at 6:00 P.M. Elizabeth created some very nice invitations for their neighbors and friends. It would be a fairly small ceremony consisting of their family and best friends that lived nearby the ranch. The children delivered the invitations on horseback, and they traveled as a group. The children were beside themselves with excitement and joy as they delivered the news.

The Russlers did, indeed, arrive at the Smith Ranch on Tuesday. There was joy and happiness throughout the ranch with everyone who was there. The Smiths had rooms for all the Russlers to have a place for to stay. The Smiths made sure that there was a comfortable place to stash their belongings in the barn. The two families grew closer together during their stay, and the ambiance was very calm and cheerful.

During their stay, Caroline's brother, John, became very interested in Philip's sister, Emily. John would stay after the wedding of Philip and Caroline on the Smith ranch. He would like to get to know Emily better. He told his parents, "I am going to stay on this ranch for awhile. I know where your new ranch is and I will come up there soon."

Chapter 14
The Weddings

Saturday finally came. The date was November 15, 1849.(17) All of the Smiths' friends, neighbors and families had gathered on the Smith Ranch to be a part of the wedding. The bride and groom were married in the newly built pavilion at 6:00 o'clock by pastor Kyle Vann.

It was a short, yet poignant, ceremony. Afterwards, they cleared the pavilion and a local group of musicians set up to play. It was appropriately a mariachi band. The music began, and everyone had a grand old time celebrating the marriage. Most of the guests danced until late into the night.

Caroline's family decided to stay on the ranch for a couple of days. They also were very anxious to move on to their new ranch. The Russler family had loaded their wagon with everything they owned. When the day came, the family was on the wagon and ready to leave for their new land. Jacob said "Remember, your place is only a one day ride from here, so please come back and visit."

Mr. Russler replied, "The same goes for you Jacob, please be our first guests when we get our house built." The Russler family left, except for Caroline's brother, John. John yelled out to his family as they were leaving, "I believe I will stay here a little longer, and I will see you soon." John had been thunderstruck by Philip's sister, Emily.

Everyone on the ranch got along famously. They all pitched in their work to help grow the cattle ranch. After a few weeks, John Russler and Emily Smith went to see Jacob and Elizabeth. John said to them, "Emily and I have fallen in love, and we would like to be married in the same pavilion that Philip and Caroline used."

Jacob looked at the two with his intense blue eyes. The wrinkles on his face were evident, and with a warm smile, he paused for a moment. "We will indeed have another wedding on the Smith Ranch and we welcome such a good man into our family," replied Jacob.

This wedding occurred within a couple of weeks and the event was just as joyful as their siblings' event. The word got to Robert and Susan, and they arrived the day before the wedding. The ceremony was very lovely and cheerful, and married by the same pastor, Kyle. John and Emily stayed for a few months on the Smith Ranch after the wedding. In the meantime, John had been inquiring about getting his own section of land in Texas.

They purchased a section of land in Mills County, near a small town called Scallorn. He and Emily prepared to leave. They were packed up and ready to leave the next day. It was with joy, as well as anxiety, that they took off for their "Promised Land." The Smiths waved to them as they rode off. The Russler couple, grinning with joy and anticipation, waved back heartily.

The couple settled the land near the small town of Goldthwaite, which is now the county seat of Mills County. It was around 20 miles northwest of where Philip and his family would settle at a later date. John and Emily developed a cattle ranch, and had three children. The Russlers worked their land for at least three generations. Philip told Caroline, "When we get settled, let's promise to visit your brother and my sister."

"I agree, and will promise that we will see them if we can," Philip said."

"There is nothing greater than family," Caroline replied.

Chapter 15
Joy

Philip and Caroline were very happy together. They had been living on the ranch for a couple of years. One night as they were retiring to bed, Caroline leaned over and gave Philip a strong kiss right on the lips. She whispered to Philip, "I'm pregnant."

Philip was shocked and delighted. He asked her, "Are you sure?"

Caroline smiled a giant smile and Philip knew that she was sure. "Oh my darling, I don't have words for how I feel" he said to her. "We will have a family and I am floating on air. The next time I go to Galveston, I will ask Doctor Steven Smith to come to the ranch and check everything out. I want this to be perfect."

They decided not to tell the family yet. They would wait until the doctor could do an evaluation. They continued their chores and Philip continued his stage coach job. He returned from his last trip and he had Dr. Smith with him. As they drove up, Caroline was standing by the porch. Philip told her "Darling, this is Dr. Steven Smith of Galveston. With my many trips and stays in Galveston, we have become friends, and he is a fine doctor."

Dr. Smith asked Caroline "Is there a bed where we could do the exam."

She grabbed his hand and said, "Certainly, come with me."

She led him into the house. Dr. Smith was carrying his medical bag. He asked her politely "Please undo your outer clothing and lay on the bed on your back. The doctor did the exam, and said, "You can put your clothes on and you and I will go talk to Philip." He reassured her that the exam went well. The two went out to the porch where they saw Philip. The doctor told Philip, "Everything seems to be in order. Caroline needs to take care of herself, eat well, and no heavy lifting."

Philip and Caroline both nodded their heads and simultaneously said, "Yes Sir!"

Dr. Smith ate dinner with Jacob's family and spent the night in the big house. There was jovial conversation, and they finally retired to their rooms. Philip told Caroline, "I am so happy, and you will make a good mother." They kissed again and had a great night's sleep.

The next morning, everyone had a hearty breakfast. Caroline asked the doctor, "Is the name 'Smith' common in Texas?"

Steven replied, "It does seem to be fairly common. Philip has told me about his journey from Germany. My parents came from England. They also changed their surname. We were "Smyth" and became "Smith" when they arrived in America. They settled in Boston where I was born."

"I grew up there and went to medical school. I also had a medical practice there. But like you folks, I heard about people moving to Texas to have their own land. I was granted a section of land about halfway between Galveston and your ranch. I rent a room in Galveston, but hope to build a house on my land and practice in the rural areas."

"We shall get together with my darling wife, Shannah. She is the love of my life. I shall see you in one month for a follow-up exam. Stay well."

Caroline replied, "Thank you and I would love to meet your Shannah, she seems charming." With that said, Philip and the doctor started out for Galveston.

Philip returned the next day. That night while in bed, Caroline said to Philip, "We need to come up with a name for our first born."

Philip said, "How about Philip?"

Caroline replied, "Well, I would like to call him 'Henry' after my mother's father?"

After some discussion, they agreed to name the child Henry Philip Smith if the baby was a boy. Caroline stated to Philip, "If the child is a girl, I would like to name her Julia Elizabeth.

Philip agreed and said, "That would be a wonderful name." They decided to tell the family that they were pregnant, and told them what they were going to name the child based on the gender. Everyone on the ranch was elated, and the news provided a happy tone around the ranch.

The months passed. Caroline told Philip, "Father, it is time."

Philip told her, "I will ask Jake to drive a wagon to the Vann Ranch and fetch Jan Vann." Caroline agreed. Philip found Jake quickly and asked him, "Hey brother, would you drive to the Vann Ranch and bring Mrs. Vann back as soon as you can?" Jake smiled and told his brother, "I'm on my way." He hooked up the wagon and took off to retrieve Mrs. Vann.

She was a mid-wife and had helped deliveries throughout the area. The ranch was only a few miles away, so he started off. Jake told Caroline, "Now don't go having that baby until I get back."

Caroline replied, "I will try not to." Jake took off and rode like the wind. He made the trip in record time and retrieved Mrs. Vann. He got back to the ranch within two hours.

Jan did her work, and the baby was delivered fairly quickly. The baby looked fine, and Philip asked his brother, "Jake, could you take Mrs. Vann back to her ranch?"

Jake said, "Sure thing Philip." He helped the mid-wife into the wagon and they took off. When he returned, he ran into the house as fast as he could to meet his nephew. Things seemed to be great. Everyone in the family would come and go and each one wanted to hold the new baby. The child was a boy and they named him Henry Philip.

Chapter 16
And Sorrow

Things around the ranch continued as normal. But, after about two weeks, Henry Philip woke up one morning with a cough. Caroline held him and felt that he was very warm. She called Philip to their room. Philip came running into the room, and with a very concerning tone asked Caroline, "Is there something wrong?"

Caroline replied with a very scared voice, "Philip! Something is wrong with the child."

Philip said, "I will go get Elizabeth, she will know what to do. I will ask Jake to ride Lightning to fetch Dr. Smith near Galveston. If we have two horses instead of the wagon, they should be able to get back today." Word got to Jake quickly. He was out bringing in stray cattle that had gotten loose. He came straight to the house.

Philip first went to find Elizabeth, then to find Jake to ask his favor. By the time Philip got back to the room, Jake was there and he already knew what he needed to do. In the meantime, Philip knew he needed to stay with Caroline and the baby. Elizabeth arrived shortly and Jake ran in and told Philip, "I'm going, right away. I will take an extra horse and we will be back as soon as we can."

Philip said, "Thanks Jake, get going."

It was an emotional day. Elizabeth had 5 children and had seen many things. She did what she could to keep the baby comfortable and found some quinine which she mixed into the milk bottle.

The baby's fever seemed to come down, but there was a great amount of worry in the family. The child had a pale color and hadn't opened his eyes much. It was difficult to get medical treatment in such an isolated place. The women would pray, and comfort the baby, and they hoped that Jake and the doctor would arrive soon.

Caroline put Henry Philip in his crib. He went to sleep quickly and she sat in a chair by the crib and rocked it gently. She would watch him and pick him up and cuddle him every few minutes. Philip stayed in the room with them and silently prayed for the baby.

After a couple of hours, Caroline picked him up again and cuddled him with love. She noticed that this time, the child seemed to be very limp. She checked to see if he was breathing, and this time he wasn't. Caroline knew that she had lost her sweet baby. She burst out with tears and cried so hard that she was quivering. Philip came to her, and Caroline almost screamed, "Philip! Our baby is gone." Philip hugged Caroline and the baby and they both were sobbing.

After what seemed to be an eternity, Philip said, "Oh darling, I'm so sorry." They lay down on their bed with the infant right between them. They lay there cuddling little Henry Philip for a very long time. About that time, Jake and Dr. Smith came through the door. It was evident what had happened. Caroline told the two, "Our precious baby is gone."

Jake said in a low voice, "I am so sorry, I should have ridden faster."

Philip stood up and said, "Jake, it is not at all your fault. The Lord takes us when it's our time. Let us pray, Heavenly Father, please take our sweet son, Henry Philip, and bless his soul, Amen."

Philip walked across the room and shook Dr. Smith's hand and said, "Doc, thank you for everything you have done and for coming out here to help."

The doctor said, "I am so sorry that I couldn't do anything for him."

Philip said, "It is late and you are tired. Please spend the night here and I will take you home tomorrow." Dr. Smith said, "Thank you, I think I will. I will tend to the child."

Philip and Caroline neither one slept at all that night. They took turns holding little Henry Philip. The next morning, they all ate breakfast and Jake had already dug a grave and put together a small cedar casket. He had also built a very nice wooden cross. He stayed up all night preparing for the day.

The family gathered in what had now become the family cemetery in the side yard. Dr. Smith had stayed for the funeral. The whole family gathered. Jacob said a beautiful prayer and they buried Henry Philip.

Philip and Caroline went to their room and cried as they held each other as tight as they could. Philip quietly told her, "We are young and we will have many children. I love you."

Caroline said, "I love you too."

Chapter 17
The Circle of Life

Philip and Caroline had stayed and helped the family run the cattle ranch for another year. The two grieved about Henry Philip every day, but rarely spoke of the loss. They wanted to have their own land, and they tried to keep their thoughts on the work they had to do each day.

In early spring of 1851, it had been almost two years since their loss of Henry Philip. On a beautiful night in early spring, Philip and Caroline retired to their bed, exhausted. When they got into their bed, Caroline inched slowly toward Philip. She finally was right next to him. He was facing away from her, but he felt her presence.

She kept getting closer and finally was pressed against his back. She put one arm under him and the other over and hugged him tightly. Philip thought, "This is kind of strange."

She whispered in his ear, "I am pregnant." Sleepy Philip wasn't sure that she said what he thought she had said. Philip asked in a somewhat confused voice, "What did you say?"

She spoke quietly, "I said, I am pregnant."

He rolled over while saying, "Did I hear what I thought I heard?" He could smell her essence and felt her warmth.

She said, "You heard exactly what I said, husband." Before he could open his mouth to say something, she brought her lips to his and they had the best kiss they had ever had.

They were both so happy and enjoying the togetherness that neither spoke. It turned into a very passionate night for the two. Being together like this and both feeling so good, their souls were somehow soothed. They fell asleep with both of them feeling like the holes in their hearts had been healed.

The next morning, the two woke at the exact same time. They were cuddling with each other in the bed. Philip asked, "Did I have the best dream I have ever had?"

Caroline told him, "That was no dream dear."

They got up and dressed, ate breakfast and did their chores. Neither one of them could get the smiles of their faces. They were going to have a baby. When they crossed paths that morning, Philip asked her, "Should we tell the family? I'm a little nervous about it."

Caroline replied, "We shall tell them at lunch. I have a really good feeling that this time things will work out.

Chapter 18
The Blessing

At lunch with the family that day, Caroline said to everyone assembled, "We have some news."

Jake said quite loudly, "Well! What's the news, lovebirds?" Philip had already spilled the beans by telling Jake the news. The two brothers had become very close. Philip replied, "We are pregnant again." Everyone cheered or whistled and they all went to the happy couple and hugged them with joy.

Everyone went back to their seats and ate lunch with smiles on their faces. The room was full of joy and laughter and everyone in the room could feel the happiness.

Caroline said, "You all know that we lost our sweet Henry Philip and we have grieved every day. It was the will of God, as it is his will to bring a new soul into our family. We both have a really good feeling about this." Philip bowed his head and said a prayer for the family and the baby that was with Caroline.

From that time forward, it seemed to invigorate the entire family. They did their chores and work with enthusiasm. Everyone seemed to be skipping around the ranch. Things became normal after a while and all was good.

In late autumn of 1851, the time had come. Philip asked Jake, "Hey brother, would you mind hitching up the wagon and summoning Mrs. Vann?"

Jake said, "Sure as shooting," and he was off like a lightning bolt.

Jake brought the mid-wife back to the ranch and it wasn't long before she helped the birthing which went well. It was a girl. That night at dinner, someone at the table asked, "So, what's her name?"

Caroline stated, "Julia." Caroline continued, "The birthing went very well and this angel was born into the world."

Caroline was holding Julia tightly with one arm and was eating with other hand. The next morning, Grandma Elizabeth started making a hand-made doll for Julia. The child was healthy and thriving. All things were good again, and the parents were filled with joy. The parents took the best care of Julia and themselves. The child had love from everyone on the ranch.

Chapter 19
It Might be a Sign

In the early summer of 1853, there came a furious hurricane that directly hit the area of the Matagorda Peninsula. (1) There were no weather forecasters at the time. It seemed liked the storm came without warning. The family had weathered several storms through the years, but had never experienced a storm like this.

The ranch was located about twenty miles from the coast with no barriers to slow the storm. Jacob and Philip were out in the pasture when they both spotted the dark gray wall to the east coming their way over the gulf. There was not a scale of hurricanes or any public communication back then. It most certainly was the strongest storm any of them had ever seen.

The storm was huge and was quickly approaching. Jacob and Philip took their horses and gathered the family and ranch hands. The men took all the animals except the cattle into the barn. That building was very sturdy. Everyone from the ranch was brought to the big house to shelter through the storm. Jacob and Philip stayed outside as the storm got closer and closer to them.

When the rain started around 10 minutes later, Jacob moved everyone to the back of the house and had everyone hunker down. Philip pulled the doors shut tightly, and the guys moved Jacob's heavy desk against the door. They had stocked the house with food and water in case of emergencies. The storm reached them and the noise was tremendous.

It sounded like a steam train passing by them closely and at a great speed. The children were terrified and the adults were trying to keep them calm. Philip realized that he had never experienced anything like this before.

Although it seemed like the storm would never end, the wind died down in about 20 minutes. Everyone went outside of the house. All of the people just stood there looking. They all scanned the ranch and saw that every building, except the main house and the barn had been leveled. Most of the fences were down also, and the cows were wandering in every direction.

Philip had read about hurricanes and said, "We are in the eye of the storm. It is a false calm, and the back side of the storm will be upon us in just a few minutes." He told everyone, "We will need to go back into the house and wait for the next wave."

Everyone returned to the rear of the house for the second event. Sure enough, Philip was right and with what sounded like a spring shower, quickly developed into the huge hurricane again. For another 40-45 minutes the onslaught of the storm continued. Finally the rain slowed down until it became a steady rain that would continue for a couple of hours.

The family emerged from their shelter in the house and looked at the devastation. The worst of the hurricane had past. All of them realized that there would be a great deal of work to rebuild the ranch.

The only words spoken were from Jacob, the patriarch of the family. "Dear ones, do not grieve or have sadness. We have all gone through so many trials and tribulations in our lives, and yet, here we are in Texas with our own cattle ranch. We will repair the big house and all of us will stay in the house as we rebuild the other structures."

"We should thank our God that none of us are dead or even injured. We are still who we always were. We will work together to restore the ranch and look forward to great times. Now everyone get some biscuits, if they are not soggy, clean up and try to have a peaceful night's sleep. Tomorrow we begin the restoration. I know we can make this ranch come back to life."

After the devastation, the community got together in fellowship. There were 10 souls that were killed or missing in the general area. Two were missing and eight were confirmed dead. The oldest man there, one of the first settlers, told the others, "Apparently there was a major hurricane as well as a tidal wave that struck us at the same time. Anyone who is willing, can join us tomorrow at dawn at The Bailey Ranch and we will search for the two missing souls."

"The funerals for each individual person will be posted at the church by tomorrow," the pastor told everyone. "Let us pray for the families who have lost a loved one." The pastor said a prayer for those who died in the storm, and when he finished, all of the people gathered said together, "Amen."

Chapter 20
Restoration and Conversation

It was an overwhelming sight to see the damage caused by the storm. It had taken so long originally to build the houses, barn, corrals, and fences. Now they knew they must start all over again. The only structures still standing were the big house and the barn. Jacob felt that even though they would have a lot of work ahead, he was so relieved that the main house and the barn were basically intact.

They all bunked down in the big house until they had rebuilt the other structures. Everyone ate a good dinner and all fell asleep early that night that first night. They knew that there was going to be major work ahead to restore the ranch and round up the cattle. Everyone except the smallest children worked as a team to methodically restore their precious ranch.

The men first built a small corral close to the house. Once it was built, they rode on horseback through the wild land and the neighbors' places. The neighbors likely would join the riders and help find and lead the lost cattle home. This chore took a long time, but the drovers found and returned most of their lost cattle.

It seemed as if the cattle had been scared by the storm, but they knew they were home. From then on, most didn't stray too far again. Jacob was very glad that he had registered a brand, and with the help of all the men had branded all of his cattle. The rounding up of most of their cattle took several days but they had retrieved most of the cattle and brought them back to the ranch. And now, the really hard work was to begin.

Jacob, Philip, and Jake, as well as kind neighbors and ranch hands began to rebuild the ranch. Elizabeth did everything she could. They first had to purchase wood and supplies. There were remnants from the storm that they could use. They began by fixing the big house and finished that up in a few days.

The next, most important project was to reconstruct the corrals and the barn so that could contain and manage the livestock. For this, they were able to salvage some of the original posts from far and near. They still needed to acquire more posts to complete the job. Jacob, Philip and the other able boys, as well as the ranch hands needed to take wagons and horses and go several miles from the ranch to gather and cut new posts.

They worked hard and it took them a few days to return to the ranch. After that, there was lots of work to do to repair the corrals. It took them a great deal of work and a few more weeks until finally the ranch was back in working order.

As it got close to the finish, the Smith children rode to all the neighboring places and invited them to a party. The party was to take place in two days. People started arriving to the Smith Ranch at the appointed time. Soon, there were many folks gathered at the ranch. The women had cooked plenty of wonderful food, the children were playing, and one of the neighbors brought his fiddle and there were happy sounds and plenty of dancing. It was a really good time for all, and the ranch was back in working order.

The town of Galveston, which is not very far from the Smith Ranch in Matagorda, was struck by a similar hurricane in 1900. It was determined to be the worst natural disaster in U.S. history. Reports state that there were at least 6,000 confirmed dead. The official estimate was between 6,000 to 12,000 people killed by the storm. The number that is cited most often is 8,000 people dead with thousands missing and never recovered.(6)

This is the city that Philip visited so often on his stage coach route, as well as the trips he made from the front line of Houston's army during the Texas Revolutionary War. It is also the city where he met and fell in love with his sweetheart, Caroline Russler.

The Smith family was extremely lucky that they all survived, and that very few people died in the area probably because it was such a sparsely populated area.

The Great Storm of 1900-Galveston, Texas(8)
Similar to the 1853 Storm of Matagorda

Chapter 21
Dinner Talk

The Smiths were very pleased and happy that they had restored the ranch completely. They were living their normal lives on the ranch and were at peace. Philip, however, was a man that had many thoughts. He was a dreamer, and yet, he was a man that made his dreams come true. The year is now 1853. He and Caroline had one child besides Henry Philip since they were married and living on the Smith Ranch. That was Julia.

He and Caroline were very content although they would talk often about having their own place. Both were very independent. One day a stranger from Galveston was passing through the ranch. As was custom for this family, they never met a stranger even if they didn't know them. The Smiths were very social, and visitors were always welcome. One evening a man rode his horse up to the big house where the family lived.

Philip was taking a short break from tending to the horses and was sitting in a rocking chair on the covered porch. The man dismounted his horse and tied the animal to the railing. Philip said "Welcome stranger, can I help you with anything?"

The man spoke, "Hello friend, you have a fine ranch here." Philip replied, "Please sit and rest your bones."

The man took a chair next to Philip and stated, "My name is Bill Rivers, but most folks call me Rusty. I am coming from Galveston and am on my way to claim my section of land in

Central Texas. I have brokered a land grant and am getting my land at a very cheap price."

Philip was very interested in what this Bill was saying. He spoke saying, "I'm glad to meet you and would like to hear more about your new purchase."

Rusty said, "I had been trying to find one of Stephen Austin's agents, and heard that one would be in Galveston for awhile recruiting settlers for the expansion of Texas. We got together a few days ago and settled on a very good deal for land in Milam County, which is in the central part of Texas. They say it is very pretty country with rivers, prairies, big trees, as well as good soil."

Philip's head was so full of thoughts, that he wasn't sure how to respond to Rusty. He paused a moment, then started firing questions at Rusty as fast as he could. "So Rusty," he asked, "Did you talk face to face with Austin's agent? Is he still in Galveston? Is there more land up there in Central Texas? Tell me about the price." Rusty basically interrupted Philip and said, "Slow down mister and relax. I will answer all your questions."

Philip realized that he was almost making a fool of himself. He slowed his brain down and asked Rusty, "Would you like a cup of coffee?"

Rusty replied, "I sure would, thanks."

Philip told him, "I'll get some right away. Would you mind if my wife Caroline could hear what we're talking about?"

Rusty replied, "I would love to meet your wife."

Philip invited Rusty into the big house and set up a pot of coffee. He asked him to have a seat and he would be right back. He started the coffee and went upstairs to get Caroline. He returned with her and they poured three cups of coffee and had a seat near Rusty.

"Rusty, this is the love of my life, my wife Caroline. Caroline, this is my new friend, Rusty."

Rusty replied, "It is so nice to meet you Caroline."

Caroline said, "So nice to meet you too Rusty." She then asked him, "Do you mind if I ask you a question?"

Rusty said, "Sure Caroline."

Caroline asked, "How did you get the nick name 'Rusty'?"

He replied, "It probably has something to do with the red hair I have. People have been calling me 'Rusty' since I was a little boy."

Philip said what he was really thinking, "Caroline, Rusty met with Stephen F. Austin's family agent in Galveston. He struck a deal with him and bought a section of land in Central Texas. He then stopped here for a rest on his way to claim his new land."

Rusty told them, "Mr. Austin passed away in 1836."(6) The family inherited the business. They have designated some trusted friends in a few towns in Texas to continue the business. We dealt with a Mr. Williams in Galveston. Caroline was immediately excited since she and Philip had been seriously talking about purchasing their own land. Sitting right here was a man who had just done that.

Philip told Caroline what Rusty had told him, and the both of them had a hundred questions to ask. After Rusty answered all of their questions, Caroline asked him, "Why don't you stay and eat dinner with the family, and you can sleep in the bunkhouse tonight. You can have a good night's sleep, eat a hearty breakfast in the morning, and be on your way."

Rusty said, "You know, I am pretty tired and I think that is a very generous offer. I think I will take you up on that."

Both Philip and Caroline said at the same time, "Wonderful." Philip told him "Come along with me and I'll

help you put up your horse and I'll show you where you can bunk down. There is a bath that's private and you're welcome to it. We will eat around six o'clock."
Caroline told Rusty, "We can talk more at dinner."
Philip went with Rusty and they brushed down the horse and put her in a stall. Then Philip showed him where to bunk down and the bathtub if he was interested. Rusty told him, "Thank you for the hospitality and you should really think about having your own great adventure. Think of having your own land and on a river, maybe."
Philip replied, "That I will."

Chapter 22
The Dinner That Changed Their Lives

Caroline and the other ladies at the ranch cooked up a great beef stew with their own beef, and the vegetables they had grown. It was Caroline's specialty. Around six, the family gathered around a very large oval wooden table. Rusty knocked on the door at just about the same time. Philip let him in and introduced him to everyone in the room.

At dinner, everyone in the room was very intensely listening to Rusty's story about moving to Central Texas. The Smiths had lived on the coast for almost two decades and they were all mesmerized by the talk of hills, rivers, prairies and big trees. During the conversation, Jacob, who is normally not much of a talker, asked Rusty, "I hear there are Indians in that part of Texas that are not so friendly with settlers."

Rusty replied, "There are indeed native Americans in the area. They have lived in that on that land for hundreds of years. They are not pleased that the white people are settling there, on what they consider to be their land. The majority of their tribes have been driven to Oklahoma and to live on a reservation.

The natives that are still in the area mostly are part of the Comanche Nation. There are still small Comanche raiding parties who are braves that avoided capture, along with their women. The raiders move from place to place without a permanent base. They are mostly trying to steal horses, which they prize. There have at times been conflicts. They are prideful warriors and one should avoid them at all cost.

There has been some trouble between them and the settlers. I just wanted you to know the danger, besides the beauty and land before you decide to move. I have heard that there have never been raids of any size, but the most common trouble involves stealing horses."

"I have a pistol, a shotgun and a rifle, and have taught myself to be a good shot with them. If you choose to go, I suggest you do the same, just in case there is trouble." You could tell that Jacob was very concerned about the possible danger if some of his family chose to move to that part of Texas. The rest of the evening was filled with joy and celebration. There was no more talk of dangerous situations. After all, the entire family had lived through a terrible hurricane.

Rusty?

Chapter 23
The Talk

The dinner and party were wonderful. Everyone had great food and interesting conversations. After dinner, the folks all gathered on the porch and had a really nice time of jokes and stories. Those who smoked cigars lit them up and everyone certainly was enjoying both the fellowship and the beautiful starry night.

The temperature was very pleasant and the sky was cloudless. This wasn't the norm, since they lived near the coast. Most nights had at least some clouds brought on by the sea breeze.

When the party seemed to be coming to an end, neighbors began saying their goodbyes and leaving to go home. Rusty stood up and said "What a wonderful evening and what great hospitality you have provided me. I feel like we have become dear friends. I thank you for everything you have done for me."

"I know where I'm bunking, and so I am heading to bed. I will be leaving for Milam County tomorrow and am so excited to see my new place and begin my adventure as a cattle rancher myself. If any of you ever make it up that way, please let me return the hospitality that you have showed me. I will never forget any one of you."

So on that note he said, "Good Night to you all, and see you at breakfast."

Philip replied, "Good night Rusty, I hope you have a great night's sleep, and I look forward to seeing you at breakfast."

The rest of the clan almost together told him "Good Night Rusty," with a few "Sweet Dreams" thrown in. Rusty left the porch and everyone except Jacob and Philip started off to get ready to for bed.

After everyone but the father and son had left, they got into a very serious conversation. Jacob started with, "You know son that I love you with all my heart. I get the feeling that you are considering moving from the ranch to Central Texas. The story that Rusty told was very intriguing about living in that part of the world. Be honest with your old man, are you seriously considering moving there?" Philip paused for a moment, and you could almost see him thinking about what he would say to Jacob.

He finally spoke and told his dad, "Caroline and I have been talking about it for quite awhile, even before Rusty came. We love you, mom and all our family. I also love this land and being a cattle rancher. We just have a strong urge to have our own land. We feel that the adventure of moving to a place that is wild is calling us. Then, there is that other thing."

Jacob looked at his son with his steely eyes, wondering what Philip was talking about before he spoke. Jacob then asked, "What other thing are you talking about son?"

Philip quietly responded, "The hurricane dad."

Jacob asked him, "What about the hurricane?"

Philip said, "We could have all been killed by that storm and I will never forget the devastation to our ranch. It was a hardship on you, me and everyone else in our family as well as our neighbors."

Jacob replied, "I agree that the ordeal was very trying for all of us, but we survived and rebuilt, and now the ranch is back where it should be."

Philip stated, "But father, we live near the ocean and the same thing could happen again without warning." The father had to agree, but he turned the conversation to his concerns about what Philip and his family might encounter if he moved inland. He told his son, "You heard Rusty, there are Indians who feel like the land is theirs. The place is not civilized. There are no sheriffs, judges, and very few people like us who live there. You would basically be on your own in a wild, untamed place. I fear for you, Caroline, and Julia. I urge you to reconsider staying here where your family is in a civilized part of Texas."

"Father," Philip said, "Caroline and I are very excited about being settlers in a place that has not been settled. It excites us both, and both of us were very affected by that terrible storm. And Dad, you of all people must know how it feels to go to a place that is truly yours, a place where you can be free, and be the master of your own domain. I want that for me also. Caroline feels the same way."

Jacob stood as did Philip, and Jacob moved toward his son and grabbed him in a bear hug, and quietly said, "Philip, you are a wise and brave man. I have always trusted your counsel, and I know that you know what you want. I will miss you greatly if you move away, but you will always be in my heart." Close up, one could see the small trail of tears on both the men's cheeks.

They unlocked their hug and Jacob asked Philip, "What will happen next son?"

Philip said, "We will go to Galveston. There are still people there who are recruiting good people to populate the state. I even hear that there is a holding company in Galveston.

Jacob asked, "Would you let me go with you in case you need some bartering skills? I can also provide assets that might help."

This time the son hugged the father and said, "Thank you dad, I would be honored if you go to Galveston with Caroline,

Jake and me." Jacob. Jr. was Philip's brother and was 15 years younger than him. Jacob, Jr. was born in Texas and he was called Jake from a small child. Jake and Philip had been talking about each getting their own land for quite awhile.

When Jacob and Elizabeth got into bed, he told her what Philip was going to do. Elizabeth stated, "I would like to go with you to Galveston. I haven't had a vacation in my life, although I have seen as much of the world as I need to. I think it will be fun for us to stay in a hotel."

Jacob gazed into his wife's eyes and said, "You know that you are the most beautiful, smart, and wise woman on this earth. I think this will be fun and relaxing to have a trip." With that, he gave her a meaningful kiss and hug, as he spoke quietly in her ear, "I love you more than you will ever know."

Chapter 24
Back to Galveston and Forward to a New Life

Jacob, Elizabeth, Philip, Caroline and Jake began packing for the trip to Galveston. The two brothers were very close. Elizabeth had decided to go with the others. If she and Jacob decided to buy some land, she would need to sign a deed also. They all would leave for Galveston in a few days.

The days passed and the day arrived for the trip. The five Smiths loaded up the wagon and left for Galveston at dawn. It was a very familiar route that Philip had driven too many times to remember. The trip was easy, and they arrived in Galveston around 4 P.M on a Monday. They booked themselves two rooms in the same hotel where Philip used to stay when he had his stage coach job.

The lady at the desk, Melissa, recognized Philip and said, "Mr. Smith, so glad to see you again and Miss Russler as well." Philip chuckled and told the lady, "Thank you Melissa, but Miss Russler is now Mrs. Smith. We have been married for a few years. We have a lovely daughter named Julia. I also would like for you to meet my father, Jacob Smith, and his wife Elizabeth, as well as my younger brother, Jake."

Melissa replied, "So nice to meet you Misters and Mrs. Smith and congratulations, Philip and Caroline. We always enjoyed your company when you stayed here. Here are your two room keys, one for the room you always stayed in, and one for the room next door for your father and mother. Jake can stay in either room."

"We hope that you enjoy your stay, and please let me or someone know if you need anything. Do you have any idea how long you might stay," asked Melissa.

Philip stated, "We are here to speak to someone from the Galveston Holding Company. We plan to inquire about buying some land in Central Texas, and plan to settle the land." Melissa, said, "The holding company is only two blocks away from the hotel on the right, and is open every week day."

Philip said, "Thank you Melissa for the hospitality and information."

They picked up their luggage and climbed the stairs to the second floor. The two rooms were side by side and it provided a wonderful feeling of nostalgia, since this was the place where Philip and Caroline met and fell in love.

They arrived on a Monday, and all agreed that they would go to the holding company first thing in the morning. Jacob, Sr. told the others that "I haven't been this excited in a long time. As a matter of fact, I don't think I've ever stayed in a hotel. We will see you for dinner. Just knock on our door around 6:00 P.M."

Philip knocked on his father's room door around six, and Jacob and Elizabeth came out of the door dressed rather well. Caroline, with her charming way, said, "Well, Jacob Smith, you look rather spiffy this evening." The three men chuckled, and Jacob blushed and said, "You know, I hardly ever wear my good clothes except to go to church. I rarely leave the ranch. This trip is just what Elizabeth and I needed. Let's go have a fine dinner and get a good night's rest. We have some business to take care of tomorrow."

The five went to the restaurant adjacent to the lobby and they found a very nice table. The waiter, Thomas, walked to their table and asked if they would like something to drink.

When he looked at the customers, he said exactly what Melissa had said, "Well, so glad to see you Philip, and you too Miss Russler."

They all had a good laugh and Philip explained to Tom, "Well Tom, so glad you are still working here. As I told Melissa at the desk, Caroline and I have been married for a few years and we have a precious daughter, Julia. I want you to meet my father, Jacob, Sr., his wife and my mother Elizabeth, and my brother Jake. We live on our family ranch near Matagorda. My father and his family moved to Texas in 1833. I was only 12 years old when we moved here."

Jacob stood up and shook hands with Tom, then sat down and said, "We would like five waters, and five of your best steaks, with all the trimmings. Also, bring us a bottle of your best wine and glasses. I feel like celebrating."

Tom left and said "I'm so glad to meet you two Jacobs, and Elizabeth. It's so good to see you again, Philip and Caroline. Congratulations on your marriage, and your child. I'll tell the cook that we have special guests and they will need the VIP treatment. I'll be back shortly." Philip said, "Oh Tom, I meant to ask you, are you still painting?" A big smile appeared on Tom's face.

Tom answered, "Yes I am. I am getting fairly well known, and a lot of people seem to like my paintings. I'm actually selling some of them. I usually paint landscapes, but I do commissions sometimes of people and animals. I actually sold a painting to a ranch lady from Montana. She was staying in the hotel and looking for a few head of cattle to improve her herd. Her name is Shirle. It was kind of odd that there was no "y" at the end of her name. She is a grand lady however, and I like the way she spells her name. Thank you for asking about me, and I will be back soon with your dinner."

The family enjoyed the dinner, and everyone was in good spirits. They were very excited about their reason for being here. When they were through eating and drinking, Jacob said to his sons and daughter-in-law. "I am so pleased to be here with you four. I am very happy to be able to help you find out what lands are available in other parts of Texas. Since you have made this decision, I will be able to help with the purchasing. The ranch has brought us money and it couldn't have been done so without your help. Raise your glasses and have a toast to the Smith Ranch and beyond."

They clicked their glasses and Philip said, "To our mom and dad!"

"We will go to the holding company first thing in the morning, after having a good breakfast. So you folks get a good night's rest and I will see you in the morning," Jacob said. They all rose and left to go to their rooms, all were experiencing an unusual sense of joy and excitement.

The next morning, the party went downstairs and sat at the same table they had eaten dinner on the night before. They were all so excited and happy. None of them knew exactly what they were going to encounter. They all ate a hearty breakfast of eggs, sausage and biscuits. They had all dressed well before going to breakfast. When they were finished eating, they left the hotel and walked the two blocks to the Galveston Holding Company. Stephen F. Austin had died in 1836, and he bequeathed the company to his wife and children.

None of the Austin family really was interested in the business, so they found managers that they trusted to run the business. Stephen F., himself, loved Texas and realized that Texas was a very large place, mostly unsettled. His goal was to help populate what was truly amazing land.

His family, especially his wife, was determined to continue Austin's dream. The company had offices in Austin, San Antonio, and Galveston. A few years after Austin's death, the family decided to sell the company. It was bought by the Williams family from New York State.

The Smiths had made an appointment with a Charles Williams, who was the manager of the Galveston branch at 10:00 A.M. They arrived a little early, making sure they were not late. The five Smiths went through the door, and sitting at a rather Spartan desk was a gentleman of middle age.

Mr. Williams stood up from his desk and announced, "You must be the Smiths from Matagorda. My name is Charles Williams, and I will be happy to speak with you folks today. I am the manager and will try to help you in any way I can. Please take a seat in front of my desk and we will get to know each other."

The Smith bunch all sat at the front of Mr. Williams' desk and Jacob stated, "My name is Jacob Smith and I would like to introduce you to my son, Philip, and his charming wife, Caroline, and my youngest son, Jake, and especially the love of my life, my wife Elizabeth. We migrated from Germany to Texas in the year 1833. We have developed a working cattle ranch and our whole family has been living and working on the ranch since we arrived."

Mr. Williams told the five that he knew about the growing territory of Texas. He was enticed to move to Texas to help the Austin family. He told the Smiths, "I actually live in New York state and have been intrigued with Texas ever since Stephen told me about it. I spend most of my time here in Texas and my family purchased the company from the Austin family.

My focus is in the central part of Texas. There is beautiful land with rivers, prairies, hills and fertile land. I have purchased land in the area myself, and of yet, I have not ever been there to see it. I am hoping that the land appreciates in value and I can make a profit."

"The part of Texas that I deal with is located in what could be described as wilderness. There have been native Indians who have lived on the land for hundreds of years. We are looking for settlers who are willing to work the land and bring civilization to that area of the state. The land is very inexpensive, and I actually have many acres available in Milam County. You told my secretary that you are interested in procuring some land of your own in that region."

Philip said "My brother Jake and I do have a very great interest in owning some land in that area."

Mr. Williams asked, "Do you have an idea about how much land you would want to purchase?"

Philip replied, "I served in the Revolutionary War, and have this document that gives me claim for 640 acres of available land for my service. Could this claim be adjacent to the land that we are to buy," Philip asked.

Mr. Williams replied, "Of course, as long as the parcel you want is available. It will be a little different than buying land, but you will have a clear deed, and it can be adjacent to your family's land. The land grant is open to you as long as you live. We will take care of that."

Philip told him, "We are cattle ranchers, and we are interested in a large amount of land so that we can continue with the cattle business. As for amount of land, it will depend on the cost of the land."

Jacob got right down to business. "Mr. Williams, how much land is available, and what would be the cost of the land we are talking about?"

Mr. Williams told them, "Since it is unsettled land, we would be able to sell the land very cheap. Depending on the size of the land will determine the cost per acre. What amount of land would you like to have?"

Philip said, "I don't know how much the land will cost, but if it's cheap enough, we would like to attain at least a few sections of land." Mr. Williams unrolled a rudimentary map of the area with parcels drawn by sections. Mr. Williams told them, "I will go next door to drink some coffee and give you folks some time to talk. I should be back in about 15 minutes." The Smiths nodded, and the gentlemen stood as the man left the office.

After he left, Jacob responded with "We will have to see what the offer is, but as you know, the larger the land, the more cattle you can run and the more profitable it will be. Let's see what Mr. Williams offers, and perhaps we can negotiate with him." By this time, the father was excited for Philip's idea. Jake chirped in, "I am also for this all the way," he said with a smile.

The folks had decided on a plan just as Mr. Williams returned to his office. After Williams sat, Jacob asked him, "What would the cost be per acre, if we were to acquire 4 sections of adjacent land?" Mr. Williams paused and looked carefully at his books. Finally he said, "For that amount of land, we can sell it to you for $0.15 per acre, minus the section for Philip which is granted to him by the Republic of Texas."

"Mr. Philip Smith has shown me a paper, signed by Stephen F. Austin. It is a land grant of one section in any part of our territory, due to his honorable release from the Republic of Texas Army. We will submit this document to the clerk and provide it with the acreage you have determined that you want. It will be done, and Philip will receive his section due to his service to Texas. You must live and work the land for five years, and cannot sell any of the land in that time period. If you meet those standards you will have a clear deed to the land."

"And, the land I'm thinking about will have fertile land, a pecan grove, a large portion of riverfront on the Lampasas River, and hills as you go west. I'm told it is very beautiful," stated Mr. Williams.

Jacob said, "Please excuse us for a minute."

Mr. Williams volunteered, "How about I take a short walk and you folks can stay in here and talk it all out? How does 10 minutes sound? I can take more time if you need it." After Mr. Williams left, Jacob, Jake, Philip, Elizabeth, and Caroline moved their chairs into a circle. Jacob, said, "The offer seems to be fair, what do you four think about it?"

Caroline spoke first, and said, "It seems like a fair price to me also, but perhaps we can negotiate it down. We will need money to build a house, barn and corrals."

Elizabeth agreed saying, "I don't really want the kids to leave, but I agree that it seems to be a very fair offer."

Jake stated, "I am with Philip, Caroline and Mom. I think we all would appreciate you being our spokesman, Dad. You are wise to the world, and have done very well with your dealings before."

Philip said, "I agree totally. Are you up for it Dad?"

Jacob, the father, with a twinkle in his eyes told them, "I will be happy to."

Mr. Williams returned to his office and they all took their places. Williams asked, "Well, what about my offer at fifteen cents an acre if you purchase 3 sections. A section of land is 640 acres".

Jacob told Williams, "We will buy the land unseen, this day, if you sell it for $0.13 per acre.(9)

Philip had been doing the math on a sheet of paper and told the group, "four sections of land equals 2560 acres. Minus my section as a grant, that would be 1920 acres to buy. At thirteen cents per acre, the total cost would be $2496."

"Well, Mr. Williams" said Jacob, "that is our final offer."

Mr. Williams paused, thinking, and said, "I accept that offer from such a good family. I must tell you before we finalize the deal something you need to know. Some of the land has been surveyed, and some has not. Down by the river, especially, the land deed will be stated by landmarks. Philip and Caroline can pick the section they want, and the county clerk will do the Land Grant paperwork. The others, you folks can sort out. We will do one price for the other three sections."

He continued, "For example, I am reading the description of a parcel deed that states, '200 yards south from the largest Live Oak tree to the middle of Lampasas River'.(3) Even though these deeds seem primitive, they have been consistently accurate in the past. If we conclude this, I will agree to have the 2560 acres surveyed for 4 sections. The surveying will be completed as part of the total amount."

They all stood up and each Smith individually shook Mr. Williams' hand, and the deal was done. In Texas, at that time, a man's or woman's handshake was their bond. Williams stated, "Today is Tuesday. I will talk to the County Clerk and try to get the deeds ready on Thursday at 10:00 A.M. I will go straight to the courthouse now, and I will drop by the hotel after I clarify it. You can make the payment at that time and the deeds will be notarized at the courthouse on Thursday."

"I want to thank you all, and I am sure that you will be well satisfied with that charming land. Our company has bonus for buyers that purchase large amounts of land. The company will give you 50 more acres at no cost. Just let me know which section you would like the additional acreage attached to, and I will tell the surveyors."

The Smiths returned to the hotel and went straight to the restaurant for coffee and tea. Everyone was smiling and happy. Jacob, however, looked a little melancholy. Caroline noticed his look and asked, "Are you feeling all right papa?" Jacob Senior said, "I am so happy that you folks are doing what you are, but I realize that I will not be seeing you very much at all, and that makes me sad." They all had a beer in celebration, and papa was smiling again.

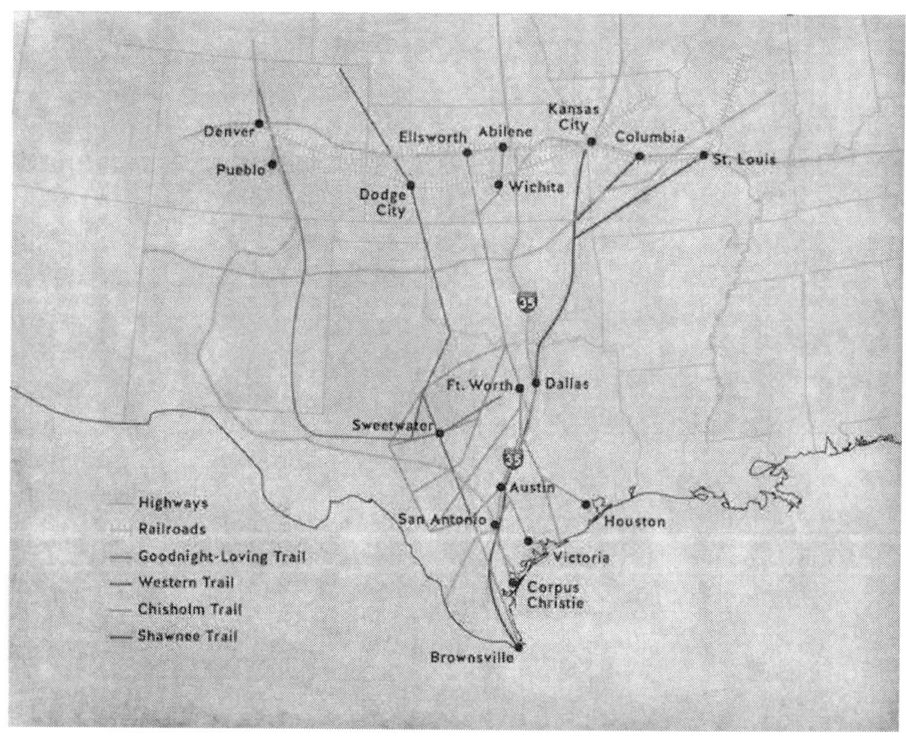

**Map of major cattle trails in Texas
in the 1800s(7)**
The land that Philip and Caroline settled on was a feeder branch
of the Chisholm Trail.

Chapter 25
Taking Care of Business

Mr. Williams had dropped a note to Melissa at the hotel, to let the Smiths know that the meeting at the courthouse will indeed be on Thursday morning at 10:00 A.M. in the County Clerk's office. Melissa left the note under one of the doors.

The day is Thursday, the day that they will close on the land deal. The Smiths got up early, as usual, and met for coffee and breakfast downstairs in the restaurant of the hotel. The folks left the hotel and walked to the courthouse. They found their way to the County Clerk's office and arrived a few minutes before 10. They saw that Mr. Williams was already in the office, and he saw them and waved them to come in.

Mr. Williams greeted the Smiths and introduced them to the County Clerk, "I would like you folks to meet Mrs. Thurman. She is a very efficient and honorable lady. She will walk us through the process and I have all of the paperwork I think I will need. Please have a seat at the round table and we can get started." Jacob, Jake, Philip, Elizabeth, and Caroline all took a seat and the business began. Mrs. Thurman's told the folks that her name was Mary Margaret, and she said, "You can call me 'Margie'."

Margie had all of the correct paperwork for the transfer of the land. She said, "I will write out the deeds, get your signatures, and notarize them in the court records. It should not take a very long time. We will start with the transfer of the money."

Jacob spoke up and said, "We have mutually agreed upon the amount of the transaction. I have brought the correct amount in cash. Jacob handed the bag to Mrs. Thurman. She counted the gold coins as Mr. Williams watched her carefully. When she was through, she stated that Jacob had brought the arranged $2496.00 for the land. Mrs. Thurman had written out a bill of sale, and she gave the money to Mr. Williams. He had watched the clerk count out loud the amount of payment as it happened. He said, "Well, that is the correct amount according to our deal."

Margie then read the bill of sale with all the specifics of the property and gave the document to Mr. Williams. He signed it, and then handed to Jacob and Elizabeth, who also signed it. Jacob returned it to the clerk who sealed and notarized the document. She told the two men, "My assistant will make one copy for each of you which will have the official seal of the county. You should be able to pick the copies up after noon tomorrow. Each landowner must sign the documents for each individual parcel. The next step will be to assign ownership to the 4 sections of land, plus the additional 50 acres. How would you like to assign each section?"

Philip told Mrs. Thurman, "The family had already discussed this, and Jacob was picked to report the assignments of the land. Jacob stated, "We would like to deed the northern most section to Jacob Smith, Sr. and wife Elizabeth. The adjoining two sections south of Jacob's land will be owned by Philip Smith and his wife, Caroline. One of those sections will be designated for the land grant deed. Caroline, who is here, can sign, if needed. Jacob, Jr. will have one section adjacent to Philip's land to the south. After discussion among us all, the generous extra 50 acres will be an extension of the two son's sections, to be 25 acres each attached to the borders of their land on the west. In this manner of dividing, all will get independent parcels of land that will have riverfront property of the Lampasas River on the eastern border of all parcels".

Mr. Williams agreed to the terms, and told the Smiths, "This concludes our transfer, I have enjoyed doing business with such a lovely family and I am quite sure that those moving to Central Texas will love your new places. Each of you will need to go by the clerk's office to get your notarized copies of the land sales and the deeds. They should be available in two days."

"As I told you, I will be dispatching a surveyor to the newly purchased land to finalize the surveys. We will give you plenty of time for you to move and get settled, but here is a map to the area. The surveyor will find you and complete the entire survey. You can have the survey deeded at the county seat. For now, I congratulate you on your new land, and I wish you all the very best. Please feel free to contact me if you have any questions, or need anything. It's been a pleasure," Mr. Williams stated.

With that conclusion, the family returned to the hotel and everyone was relieved as well as happy. That night at dinner, everyone was in a jovial mood and Jacob spoke and said, "Well you folks have already had many adventures, but you boys and your families are in store for many more."

Elizabeth stated, "I honestly can't believe everything that we have been through to get here. It seems like such a distant memory of our farm in Germany. I want to tell each and every one of you how proud your papa and I are of you."

Philip was next and declared, "Mom, Dad, Caroline and Jake, I am so proud to be a part of this wonderful and brave family, and I am quite sure that we all have been blessed."

Jake held his beer in the air and quietly shouted, "Here is to the Smith family may they live and love for a long, long time!" They all brought their glasses together and all at once cried "Cheers!"

The next day, the family toured Galveston and Philip had planned a surprise. He had two wagons ready to go for a short trip. Caroline and he were the only ones who knew where they were going. They all went to the stable where the two wagons and horses were ready. Caroline rode with Philip, and Jake would drive the other wagon with Jacob and Elizabeth. Jake asked Philip, "Where are we going, big brother?"

Philip replied, "It's a short drive. I am taking you to the place where I had an epiphany, and my mind had never been clearer. It was a moment in time when I knew what my future would be and what I must do to achieve it. Just wait, we will be there soon." Philip retraced his tracks with Lightning to the wooded spot that he had visited. After a few minutes, everyone could see the small clump of trees and a running creek.

Philip and the others arrived and they pulled the wagons to the edge of the small forest, and tied the horses to the nearest trees. They all got off the wagons at the same time. Philip told them, "Just follow me into the woods." They followed and stopped at the place that he and Lightning had been before. Philip said, "Please have a seat everyone."

They all sat on the lush grass next to the rolling creek.

"I thought this would be the perfect place to assimilate all our thoughts, feelings, and behaviors that we had all experienced in the last week and a half. We have certainly enjoyed each other's company," Philip said. He had brought a bag with fruit, nuts, cheese and a bottle of wine. He passed out the glasses and offered the food to all of them.

"Let's celebrate this moment and count our blessings with a toast," said Philip. They all had a glass of either wine or the pure sweet water of the creek. They put their glasses together, and in unison and clinked their glasses and cried out, "Cheers."

They talked and laughed and wandered around Philip's enchanted spot while they snacked on the food he had brought. Philip next asked them all "Please sit back down and be very quiet." After a few moments of silence they all noticed the cottontail bunny hopping near the creek. Then they saw the Blue Heron swoop down and land in the middle of the creek. The family was thrilled to see nature with wildlife in their natural environment.

Philip said, "It is getting late and I feel like we should mount up and head for home. Make sure that you look up on the return journey, you might just be surprised." Soon after everyone was loaded on the wagons, they were pulling out of the wooded spot, then, without a word, Philip pointed the index finger of his right hand towards the sky. They all looked up at where he was pointing, and flying low in all his magnificence, was a soaring Red Tailed Hawk.

They were very quiet on the trip back to the ranch. Each had seemed to have gained some kind of a crystal understanding of the universe, and they all realized that they were a part of it. The ride back was joyful.

Chapter 26
Planning for the Adventure of their Lives

When the party returned to the ranch, all of them were exhausted, both physically and emotionally. When everyone had unloaded the wagons and themselves, Jacob told them, "Well, family, that was quite an experience, but look at the outcome. Our two sons and their families will be having the adventures of your lives. I think that the best thing we can do right now, is to have some food and retire to our beds and gain our energy back." That is exactly what they all did, and they all slept like babies until the next morning.

The next morning, all of the Smiths sat down in the large, oval table made of oak. It was large enough to seat the whole clan. The table could oblige 12 people. The Smiths gathered in the big house around 7:00 A.M. for breakfast. Elizabeth and Caroline had risen quietly and had been preparing breakfast since around 5:30 that morning. They planned to make the best breakfast feast they could with the food they had on hand.

The ladies had bought some fruit on the way home and had cooked fresh biscuits. They sliced the fruit and made the best omelet a person could eat. They had made the biscuits and the biscuits were about ready to come out of the oven. The odor was fabulous. Every member of the extended family took a seat as the clan dribbled in to the dining room.

The adults were drinking coffee and the children were drinking fresh milk. The children had squeezed the milk from the cows in the barn. Besides being a cattle ranch, the family also had farm animals, such as chickens, pigs, and four milk cows. The animals allowed them to have fresh meat, chickens, pork, eggs, and fresh milk most any time they wanted.

Everyone was sitting at the table and Caroline stepped into the dining room with joy in her voice and stated, "O.K. family, breakfast will be served very soon." The girls old enough to help the women headed for the kitchen. The table had already been set. Elizabeth, Caroline and the girls began to bring the hot food and place it on the table in platters and bowls that were very large.

They started passing the food, and each person would dish out their portion. Next they would pass each platter down the line until everyone got their breakfast. Before eating a meal, the family would always have someone give a blessing. Philip spoke up and said, "Could everyone please bow your heads?"

He continued with, "Dear Lord, please bless this food, and all those that helped prepare it. Thank you for our health and please bless this beautiful family that you have provided. Please bless those that will be moving from this ranch, and for those that stay. Bless the travels to come. Heavenly Father, please grant us health and happiness, peace and love, and the power of your Holy Light, now and forever, in the name of Jesus Christ, Amen."

Everyone else echoed "amen" roughly at the same time. Elizabeth then spoke, "Enjoy and dig in." That they did.

There were several conversations going on as they ate their breakfast. Jacob, Elizabeth, Philip, Caroline, and Jake purposely sat together. Jacob said, "Well folks, looks like you will be leaving us soon."

Jake replied, "Dad, mom, and our other relatives and friends, on behalf of me, Philip, Caroline, and Julia, thank you for all your help and financial and emotional support. We will all miss you and the ranch, but rest assured that we are going to have the times of our lives."

Philip added, "Yes, indeed brother, we are soon going to have the greatest adventures of our lives. Mom and Dad, we hope that you two will come visit us. And we promise that we will all try to come down from time to time."

Jacob spoke, and said, "Your journey will be difficult, and settling your new land will require a great deal of work, danger and hard times. It also will serve you love, joy and honor. We will try to come see your new places, and certainly want you to come back as often as you can. Words can't say how much we love you and will miss you. We are so proud of all of you. Jake, you were too young to really remember us settling this place. Philip, you do remember the hardships, as well as the joy, don't you"

Philip spoke is a quiet voice, "Yes, father, I remember it well." Philip was twelve years old when the family settled the place in 1833. He worked with his father to build the ranch and had been a very important part of it. (8)

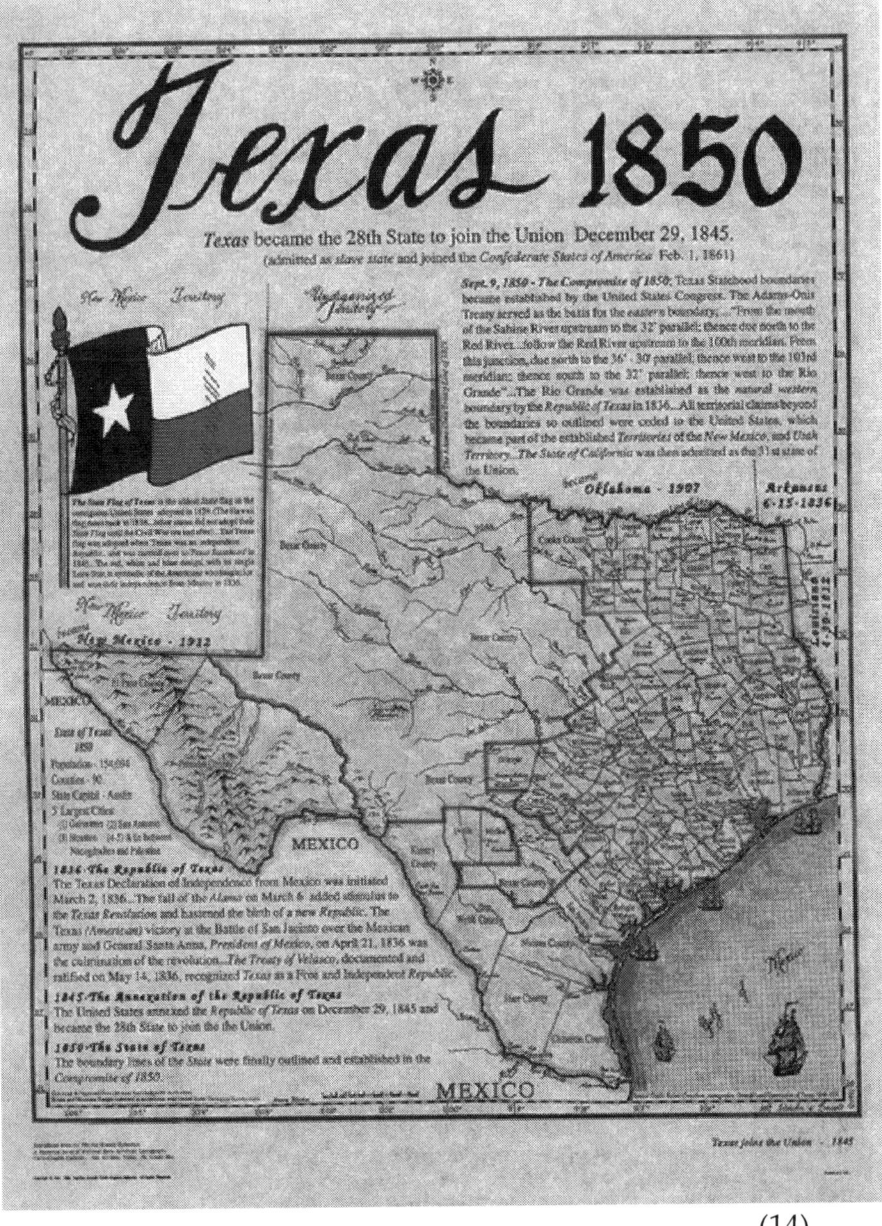

Texas 1850
Texas became the 28th State to join the Union December 29, 1845.
(admitted as slave state and joined the Confederate States of America Feb. 1, 1861)
MEXICO
MEXICO
MEXICO

(14)

Chapter 27
Preparing to Leave

Philip, Jake and Caroline began in earnest packing for their trip to Central Texas. Jacob, Elizabeth, and the children who were old enough, all worked very hard to help get things ready. Philip, along with Jacob, listed the things that they must have as well as what they could take if they had room. They made the list, and each day they worked toward getting themselves ready.

Part of their 'must have' items included two wagons, four oxen, and plenty of dry food and water. They also began packing their clothes, two tents, tools they might need, and blankets and pillows. They took money in the manner of gold coins, which were hidden so well that no one could find them except the people on the trip. Only they knew where the coins were hidden. Jake and Philip each carried a rifle, a shotgun, and a revolver.

Caroline also carried a small hand gun for self defense. Philip and Jake made sure there was enough ammunition for all the weapons to last for months. They had no idea what kind of situations they would encounter.

The men had built a hidden compartment of the bottom part of the floorboard on one of the wagons. They would hide their money in this place. It was actually very clever. They removed a section on a bottom board and replaced it with a board that could be removed. It looked like the original board. It had tongues and grooves in both ends with which they could secure it. They would have to seal the safe before crossing a river.

After several days of packing, re-packing, inventories checked off, and conversations among them made them feel like there were well prepared. They chose May 15th as the day they would leave.

Gold Coins common in Texas in the 1850s

Philip went to Caroline with an anxious face. He said, "I have been thinking, and I know in my heart that I need to take Lightning with us. I love that horse and want to have him with me. Caroline smiled the sweetest smile and held him tight. She told Philip, "He must go with us."

There were a few days left before they would start their journey. Philip called Jake aside and asked him, "I truly want Lightning to go with us."

Jake replied, "We have enough time, I think you and I need to go to Galveston and get that horse, if we can. We can ride on two of our best horses and you can get your horse." Let's mount up and go right now. We can ride straight through the night, get the horse and come right back."

Philip asked Jake, "What if he won't sell him?" Jake told his brother, "We have to have faith, let's make it happen." Philip agreed and the brothers told Caroline what they were doing and they took off. The boys rode all night long. They pushed their horses and only stopped to rest and drink water. They arrived in the early morning in Galveston. When the boys got to Galveston they went straight to the stables.

When they arrived they saw Bobby and told him that they needed to talk to Wade as soon as they could. Bobby sensed their urgency and said, "I will go to Mr. Wooten's ranch and try to fetch him." He took off to the Wooten Ranch. He said, "I will be back as soon as I can." Bobby took off and Jake told Bobby, "We will handle the stables, you just get going and thanks for doing this."

The brothers settled in at the stables and took care of what was needed. It was about an hour when Bobby and Wade arrived at the stables. The two men came in and Wade saw the Smith boys and asked, "What is so important to call me to my stables so urgently boys?"

Philip got right to it. He told Mr. Wooten that he wanted to buy Lightning to go with them on their journey. The horse was looking straight at Philip the whole time. Philip asked Wade, "Would you sell Lightning to me? I love that horse and I couldn't imagine going to settle in Central Texas without him. I think he loves me too."

Wade stood there and soaked in what had just been heard. He told Philip, "I know of the bond that you and Lightning have, and I have never seen a man and horse so fond of each other. Yes, I will sell you Lightning."

Philip said, "Well Wade, I thank you for being willing for me to buy Lightning. How much would you need for the horse?"

Wade said, "I'm not sure, again, I have never seen a man who loves a horse as much as you do this one. He belongs with you. You and Lightning need to be with each other."

Philip asked Wade, "How about I trade this horse for Lightning?"

Wade took a long detailed look at the horse and said, "That's a deal. That horse looks like he will be a good coach horse." Philip shook on it, and then he went over and hugged

Lightning. It was as if Lightning knew what was happening. He whinnied and danced in his stall. Mr. Wooten wrote out a bill of sale and ownership for Philip Smith.

They both signed the paper and Bobby signed as a witness. He also wrote a separate document giving Mr. Wooten possession of Philip's horse, Ranger. They also signed the second document. With a hand shake, the deal was complete. Philip said to Wade, "I thank you so much, and you will never know how pleased I am."

Wade stated, "I think we have done great thing today and I am glad to be a part of it. I will miss you and wish you boys the best of luck on your journey and your new home". Philip shyly spoke to Wade and said, "I guess I need to resign from the company, and please know that I have enjoyed working for you."

Wade replied, "We will miss you and you were the best driver I have ever had. Philip got Lightning ready and he and he rode the horse back to the ranch with Jake. They were home before dark. Philip was a very happy man. All was right in the world.

Chapter 28
The Day Arrived

The day was May 15, 1854 in the early morning. The wagons were loaded and were in good shape. The oxen and horses were fed and watered, and appeared to be in good health. The entire family and all the ranch hands gathered outside the big house to say their farewells. There were hugs and kisses all around. It was unusually quiet. They all knew that this was going to be a very difficult emotional time, with joy as well as sadness.

Jacob and Elizabeth and the children knew that staying at the ranch without their kin would be sad for a time. The adventurers were sad also, but they had the overwhelming feeling of excitement and joy. After all, they were about to embark on a once in a lifetime adventure. They were prepared and very excited to get started. Jake was 18 years old and Philip was 33.

After the hugs, Philip, Caroline and daughter Julia climbed on one of the wagons. Jake boarded the other wagon. They had a map showing their itinerary. Maps like this were rudimentary because they were drawn by scouts and Mexican natives who had been in the country they would be settling in.

The travelers would take a course north to northwest. They would go through LaGrange, Bastrop, Austin and Round Rock. From there, they would head northwest to get to their land that would someday become Lampasas County.

Jacob, Sr., Elizabeth and their children huddled around the wagons. Tears appeared on everyone. Some had tears of sadness, others had tears of joy, but most had both. Philip broke the silence with, "We are such a fortunate and happy family. We will see you again, but this is something that we were meant to do."

Jacob replied, "If ever there was a strong family that could make a journey like this, it is you folks."

With that being said, Philip and Jake cracked whips over the oxen and they started off into the great unknown. The two wagons had gone about 100 feet. Julia started yelling as loud as she could, "Dolly!, Dolly!" Philip and Jake reined in their oxen and came to a stop.

Philip asked Julia, "What is wrong, Julia?" Julia replied, "I left Dolly, I need to take her with me."

Dolly was a handmade doll that Elizabeth had made for Julia when she was just three weeks old. It was made with love and great care. Julia was now 3 years old, and almost 4. Julia had slept with Dolly every night of her life. When Julia shouted out "Dolly," Elizabeth knew right away what was happening.

She had already started to run to the house to retrieve Dolly from the front porch. She was walking back to the wagon with the doll. Elizabeth gave Dolly to Julia and said, "Here is your little friend sweetheart." Julia grabbed it and crushed it against her chest as tight as she could.

She gave her grandma the biggest hug and told her, "Thank you grandma, I would cry every day if I didn't have Dolly."

They both cried with joy. Julia said, "Thank you for bringing me Dolly. I will think about you every night when I go to bed. I love you so much grandma." The wagons, cattle and folks left Matagorda to find their 'Promised Land'.

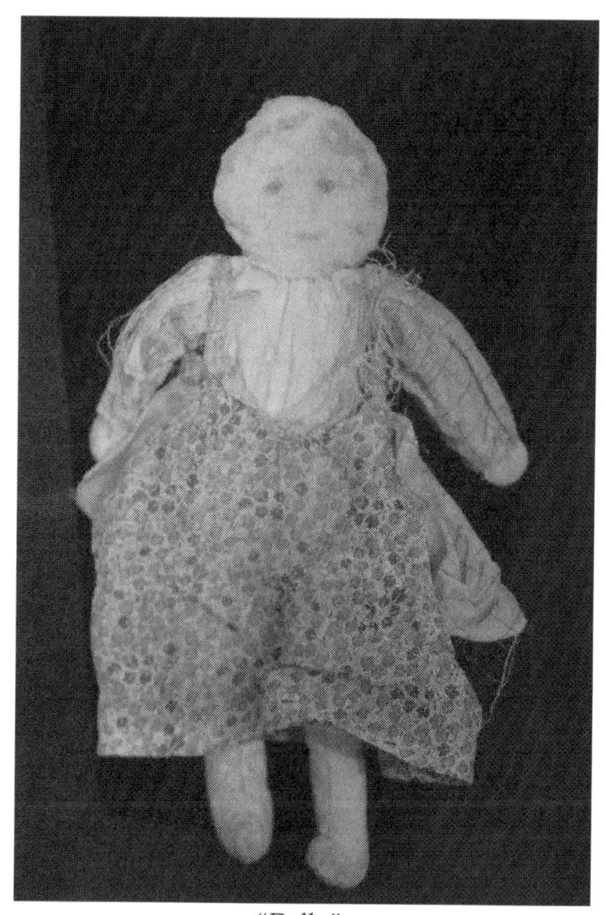

"Dolly"

Chapter 29
Adios for Now

Behind each wagon, there were two horses tethered to each wagon. One of the horses behind Philip's wagon was his beloved Lightning. Besides the horses, Philip and Jake had hired three Mexican cattle drivers for the trip. The brothers were taking a small herd of around twenty head to start the cattle ranch. When Jacob first started a cattle ranch he owned mostly Herefords from England.

By the 1850s, however, the cattle drives had driven Longhorn cattle from Mexico and soon there were many in Texas. The cattle that Philip and Jake were taking had some purebred Longhorns. There were also mixed breed cattle from Jacob's ranch.

It was quite a sight to see the convoy heading north from the Smith Ranch. Standing and waving good-bye, Elizabeth was leaning on Jacob's shoulder, crying from a mixture of sadness and joy. She couldn't see Jacob's face. If she had seen his face, she would have seen the biggest grin that he had ever had. See also would have seen some tears running down his cheeks.

Jacob was full of joy and pride when he watched his sons with Caroline and Julia begin the journey. He would never tell Elizabeth, but in his mind he longed to be with them. He was always a brave man with curiosity, and love of adventure. He knew in his heart that the sons that just left, possibly forever, were men of his own cut. His smile got even bigger.

Oxen Wagons in 1850's Texas

Chapter 30
The Journey Begins

The settlers had had about 280 miles as the crows fly to reach their destination. The journey had very few real roads, and they mostly would go through meadows, rocks, creeks, rivers, and hills as well as dealing with inclement weather on their trip. Due to the difficulties they had, the trip took 4 months to get from Matagorda to their destination. Sometimes they would only make 2 to 3 miles a day, due to the conditions. They made several stops during the drive due to situations.

The family took off from the Smith Ranch in the two oxen wagons. Julia was squeezing "Dolly" as close to her chest as she could. The first stretch actually had a dirt road that would last for a few miles. Everything seemed to be fine. As they would do throughout the journey, they would drive their wagons until it was a little before dusk, then make camp. Hopefully the camp site would be near the water of a creek, river, lake or spring.

The first night, they had made good distance and they stopped nearby a creek. The drovers would gather the cattle and Philip, Jake, and a couple of cowboys would cut or find branches that could be used as stakes. They would build a makeshift corral of rope with a combination of tying the rope to trees and the stakes. The men would make the rope taut except for a link that could be opened or closed. They would drive the cattle, oxen and horses into the corral. After all the animals were inside, the men would tie up the opening.

The vaqueros had brought their own camping gear. Their names were, Antonio, Pedro and Jose. The Smith family had two large tents made of canvas. The first thing they would do after setting up the temporary corral was to pitch the tents. The drovers pitched their tent by the cattle, oxen and horses. The vaqueros wore hand guns and each had a rifle. This untamed territory could be dangerous.

Next, everyone would gather wood and start a campfire. Caroline and one of the men would prepare something to cook over the fire. The drovers would sit around the fire and eat with the family. Caroline and a helper would cook enough for everyone to get full. The Smiths thought of the drovers as family, and they felt the same way about the Smiths.

On the first night when everyone was sitting around the campfire, Philip asked Antonio to tell them some things about themselves. Philip asked in Spanish, of which he had taught himself fairly well. Antonio was pretty good with his English as well. He replied, "Pedro is my brother, and Jose is my cousin. We have families in Monterey, Mexico. We have been in this area for about two years. When we get paid for our work, we keep enough to live on and wire the rest home to our families. We have always been cowboys, or 'vaqueros' in Spanish. We love horses and cattle as well as good people," he added.

Jake speaking in English, said, "Welcome to our family and we shall have a great adventure together." Antonio translated Jake's words to his brother and cousin. They all nodded and smiled. Most evenings, they would practice English and Spanish. They practiced hard but sometimes they would laugh out loud at the speaker's pronunciation.

With the slow moving wagons, the conditions of the ground they crossed, and driving the cattle, they realized it probably was going to take a while to get to their destination. The first few days were not remarkable.

They had a compass and the sun as their guides. Philip also had a sextant. He was interested in many things, and he had learned about navigation when he crossed the Atlantic Ocean. He would ask a shipmate often to show him how to read it. And he became quite proficient in using it. He had purchased a sextant a few years back. Also, there was the North Star at night that could help guide them as long as the sky was clear.

After traveling a couple more days, the weather had gotten difficult for travel. It started raining hard, then drizzled and rained for the next three days. Traveling had slowed to a crawl. It continued to rain and the next day they had to stop at a creek they needed to cross. It had rained so much that the creek was swollen, and they knew they would have to stay where they were until the rain stopped and the creek had gone down.

They pitched the tents and settled into the camp knowing that they would be there a while. It was difficult to find dry wood and kindling for their fire. They gathered both wet wood as well wood that was damp. Sometimes they would find fairly dry wood under a large tree near the trunk. They also had the foresight to stash kindling and dry grass in one of the wagons.

They placed the wet wood in tents to allow it to dry out. They also found a dry spot where they put the damp wood. Once they were able to get a fire stated, they moved the wet wood and set it next to the fire. It would soon be dry enough to put on the fire. In the meantime, everyone stayed in the tents and ate preserved foods such as hard biscuits, jerky, and some of the fruit that was still good.

With the creek flowing fast, they knew they would have to stay there until the rain stopped. The next afternoon, they got a small fire started under a giant live oak tree to hopefully keep it somewhat dry. The rain had dwindled into drizzle and things looked like it was going to work. On the next day the rain finally stopped. The men kept the small fire burning.

The next day was a blessing. The Sun rose at dawn and the day became a wondrous sight, with not a cloud in the sky. The wood dried out and they were very pleased.

On their journey, two men would usually take their rifles in the early morning or late afternoon and hunt for game. Sometimes they would come back with a deer, rabbit or even a squirrel. One hunter would take a shotgun just in case they saw dove or quail. They all also knew which plants and berries were edible and harvested them. Deer were fairly rare, but they did bring some back a few times. Deer were very tasty and the skin could be treated into clothing.

They would butcher whatever game they might have, and they had an old fashioned way of preserving the meat. They had a tub in the back of one of the wagons, and they would bury the meat under salt in the tub. This kept flying insects as well as most crawling critters from getting to the meat for several days. They all knew when the meat was spoiling and, if so, they dumped it. They would then wash the salt with clean water, and let it dry in the Sun. They carried salt with them the entire way.

After two days of sunshine and no rain, the party felt like they could get across the creek safely. Philip told everyone "Load up the wagons, we will be crossing the creek tomorrow." This process needed care. Lots of things could go wrong.

The water in the creek was receding, yet the current was still running a little fast. The creek was also deeper than normal. To get the wagons and gear across safely they made a plan. They decided that each person would carry important items to the other side to keep things dry. Then one driver would slowly and carefully proceed to enter the creek where they had previously scouted out the safest path. The first wagon would go across and on to high ground. The people whom carried the items spread the wet items on the ground in the sunshine. They loaded the carried items that were dry back into the wagon.

Since there were two wagons, the process was the same with the second wagon. After the wagons and passengers were safely across, they would drive the wagons ahead at least 100 feet and stop there. Next, the drovers along with Philip and Jake, would mount their horses and drive the cattle across gently and slowly.

They never knew if one or more of the cattle might get spooked. That could be a problem. In this case, the cattle were calm and gently guided by the cowboys that drove them across without incident.

Everyone in the party knew their job and they performed them perfectly as a team. When the wagons were loaded, and the vaqueros had the cattle in control, the caravan would proceed on their way north. That day and the following few days went well. They had traveled through fairly smooth and level ground.

They were hoping to reach the first real town on the trip, LaGrange. Philip and Jake guessed that with no big problems, they should reach LaGrange within a week. All was good at this point in time, and therefore, everyone was happy.

The group moved along at a reasonable rate. At the campfire during one of the stops, Jake said, "When we get to LaGrange, I will be so ready to have a real bath, sleep in a bed, and have a meal that we didn't have to make. Hopefully we will have a letter from Dad and Mom." There is a pony express that goes from Matagorda to LaGrange. Dad told us that they will try to have a letter waiting at general delivery in LaGrange.

Everyone on the trip was in good spirits. Philip said "Being in a town can renew one's spirits. But sometimes cities draw folks that can be bad. I am also looking forward to doing all the things you mentioned, Jake."

Philip had gotten a glance of two riders that seemed to have been following them during the day. He was concerned that they might come into our camp with ill intent. He was a little unsettled. He told Jake what he had seen. Jake said, "For the time being, I think we should have a lookout while at camp. I will take the first shift this evening.

They stopped their wagons near some water and pitched their tents. The wranglers pitched their tent near to the cattle. They started a fire at the main camp, and Caroline and others started preparing dinner.

Typical camp on a cattle drive

Chapter 31
There might be Bad Guys

It seemed like any other night until two masked riders came galloping into their camp. They stopped on a dime, and each shot a single round from their rifles into the air. The one in front yelled, "This is a robbery. I want everyone to throw their guns on the ground and don't say a single word. This shouldn't take very long and we will be gone. I must remind you that you shall not say anything." The two dismounted their horses with their rifles in their hands and revolving hand guns on their gun belts.

Julia turned her head and whispered to Philip, "What is happening dad, I'm scared."

The talking bandit said in a very serious tone, "Little girl, did you hear what I said? To repeat, I do not want any of you to say a single word, or we will shoot someone. Do you understand what I'm saying?" Julia looked quickly at the bandit and nodded. Then she ducked her head into her father's chest. Philip put both his arms around her to calm her. She was terrified.

The talking bandit began rummaging through the wagon as his partner had his rifle aimed at Philip. When he was through with the first wagon, he proceeded to the other. He had pulled out some things, but had not found the coins that were very well hidden. Jake and the cowboys had not been seen by the robbers, but they had heard the shots.

It was getting pretty dark and the three cowboys had silently approached the camp and had spread out, rifles loaded and pointed forward. Jake had also heard the shots and knew what was happening. Jake was on the other side from where the cowboys were, in the woods. Jake and the vaqueros were all moving quickly and silently toward the camp.

When the four were very close, unknown to the bad guys, they had surrounded the bandits. With all guns pointed at the thieves, Antonio yelled out, "Drop you guns hombres, or we will drop them for you!" The robbers looked at each other, then looked around and realized that there were four guns pointed directly at them. They dropped both their rifles and handguns on the ground.

Philip and Caroline picked up the bad guys' guns. The talking bandit asked, "What now?"

Jake told him, "We will keep your guns and turn them into the sheriff in LaGrange. You can go, but never come back to our camp. We will be watching and ready next time." Philip went over to the bandits and one at a time, pulled the masks off their faces, and told his folks, "So this is what cowards look like."

They kept the robbers' guns, and let the bandits go. Philip popped the flank of the talking bandit's horse, hard. The horse bucked, and took off in a full gallop. The other guy took off right behind his boss. When the bandits got about a hundred feet away, everyone except Julia fired shots in the general direction of the bandits. They purposely fired without hitting the bandits. They simply wanted to put an explanation mark on the incident.

With the bandits long gone, the whole group gathered around the campfire. Philip spoke and said, "Well you old gunslingers, it looks like we can defend ourselves." They all started laughing. Jake said, "I want to thank Antonio, Jose, and Pedro for helping us in a tough situation. We couldn't have thwarted those bandits without you fellows. We hired you guys as cowboys and you stood up when we needed you for something else."

Antonio, who generally spoke for his relatives stated, "Well, Smith family, we have come to like you and respect you. We are honored to be on this journey and want you to know that we are with you all the way."

Philip replied, "We feel the same way about you and are very fortunate to have you on our side, and will never forget you three vaqueros, Gracias."

They ate a great meal and opened the beer that they had brought along for special occasions. They laughed and had a great time for hours. Philip, the serious one said, "We have learned that this country is not civilized yet and there are possible dangers at any moment. I suggest that we start having a shift for the men sleeping. We will probably be safer if we have at least one man who is awake and guarding the situation." Jake, Antonio, Jose, and Pedro got together and touched clenched fists and all agreed to do their part.

Philip said, "I will take the first shift and you all can go ahead and get some sleep. Jake, you can take the second shift, Jose, the third, Antonio the fourth, and Pedro the last shift. That way, we will be guarded for the entire night."

Jake replied, "I believe we will all sleep better with this plan."

Everyone but Philip went to their tents and went to sleep. It had been quite a day and night. They all slept well, with the guard shift working perfectly, and they all fell right to sleep after each shift, dreaming about having a bath and sleeping in a bed the next day.

Chapter 32
Reaching civilization

The next day, the family and cowboys arrived in LaGrange, Texas after a long day's journey. The group headed down the main street and stopped at The Hotel LaGrange. Philip and Jake got off their wagons and went into the hotel.

The two went to the reception desk and spoke to a charming young lady. Philip said, "We need two rooms, one for my wife, our daughter, and me. We also will need a room for my brother, Jake. We will stay tonight and maybe tomorrow night as well. Our daughter could sleep in Jake's room."

The desk clerk stated, "Welcome, and please sign in. My name is Kristin Elise, but everyone calls me Krissie. It is a nickname I've had all my life. It's the name that most people I know call me by."

Philip told her, "We have traveled from Matagorda by oxen wagons and have a small herd of cattle. We are the Smiths, and we are on our way to settle land in Central Texas where we will become cattle ranchers."

Krissie said, "You all must be very tired. Here are the keys to rooms 6 & 7. You folks figure out who sleeps where, any combination will be fine. As for the wagons and cattle, there is a small ranch on the left of this road right outside of town. Mr. Hodges has a small ranch and he will let you keep your animals and wagons for a small fee. He is a very fine man. Do you have drovers with you?"

Jake answered, "Yes, we have three cowboys with us."

Krissie stated, "Mr. Hodges also has a place for the cowboys to eat and sleep, and there is also a bath that they can use."

Philip said, "Thank you Miss Krissie, you have been very helpful. We will get my wife, Caroline, and our child, Julia and bring them in. They can get to their room and have a bath and a change of clothes. Jake, I, and the drovers will take care of the animals and the wagons. "

Krissie told them, "Please let me know if you need anything, and again, welcome to LaGrange, Texas."

Philip and Jake went to the wagons and helped Caroline and Julia down and escorted them into the hotel. While Philip was checking in, Krissie noticed Julia. She made eye contact with her, and Krissie asked the little girl, "What is your name cutie?"

Julia replied shyly, "Julia." Krissie asked, "And how old are you?" Julia held up four fingers and boldly said, "three." As many young children do, she had just turned 4, but was used to saying she was 3. Krissie then told the child, "I have a 5 year old girl named Ruthie."

Julia said, "What a pretty name." Krissie was moved by young Julia. She had an idea while Caroline and Julia were standing by the desk. Krissie asked Caroline, "Would you mind if I give Julia a piece of candy?"

Caroline nodded and answered, "That would be fine, I am sure she will love it." Krissie reached under the desk top, pulled out a wrapped piece of hard candy and handed it to Julia. Julia was ecstatic. She grabbed the candy, unwrapped it, licked it for awhile, chewed some, and ate it down. Caroline said, "What do you say?"

Julia smiled and said, "Thank you Miss Krissie."

Jake left the hotel and walked back to the herd. He told Antonio, "We have found a place where you guys can bunk, and have a bath and food. The rancher can hold our cattle, oxen and horses while we are in town. We can also leave the wagons there. Philip and I can drive the wagons out there, and you guys can drive the cattle behind us." Antonio replied, "Si Jefe, vamanos amigos."

Chapter 33
A Bath and Some News

Caroline and Julia went into the hotel, got the room key from Krissie and went to their room. They took a hot bath together and soaked for a good while. When they got out and dried off, the two put on some clean pajamas and lay down on the bed and quickly went to sleep. Everyone was exhausted

Caroline was pregnant before the settlers left. She had not told Philip, because she knew that he would delay the trip until the baby was born. She also knew that they would have to wait until the baby had gotten old enough to travel.

Caroline never lied to Philip, but in this case, she knew she was tough enough to make the trip. Caroline thought of it was not really lying, but just not telling him until the time was right. She planned to break the news soon. She did not want to be the one that delayed the journey.

Meanwhile, the brothers brought everything they needed for the family's stay, and brought the things into the lobby. Philip told Antonio, "You guys can unload your stuff when we reach the ranch." They drove the wagons and the small herd out of town and headed for Mr. Hodges' ranch. It was about one mile outside of town. They stopped at the gate and a man walked out to meet them.

Philip and Jake got off the wagons and walked to the gentleman. They shook hands with Mr. Hodges as he asked, "What can I do for you folks?"

Philip replied, "We need to corral these animals, and there are three cowboys that need a bunk and a bath. The cowboys will stay tonight and maybe tomorrow night also."

Mr. Hodges told them the rate, which was very fair. "You're welcome to stay as long as you wish, and I hope you get to know my precious wife, Dianna. She is attending a committee meeting regarding 'The Arts in LaGrange'. She is very committed to making this town better.

Mr. Hodges opened the gate and the men drove the cattle through and into the corrals. The three cowboys got what they needed off of the wagon and headed to the bunkhouse. Jake and Philip stowed the wagons and sheltered the oxen and the extra horses. As they were leaving on horseback, with Philip riding Lightning, they waved at Mr. Hodges and the cowboys as they rode off. The others waved back at them. The brothers headed for town.

When they arrived at the hotel, they tied their horses on the rail and went into the hotel. Krissie said, "Your wife and daughter are in room 6 and here is the key to room 7. As the brothers were climbing the stairs, Philip asked Jake, "Hey brother, could you do me a favor?"

"Sure" said Jake.

Philip replied, "Would you mind if Julia bunks on the extra bed in your room? I would kind of like to sleep with my wife alone tonight?"

"Of course, but make sure she brings Dolly with her," Jake said glibly. And both men laughed. Philip knocked on the door 6, and Caroline and Julia cheerfully opened the door and hugged Philip and Jake. Jake asked, "Hey pumpkin, how would you like to bunk in my room tonight?"

Julia blurted out "Yay!" She grabbed Dolly and her satchel and the Philip was exhausted and filthy. Caroline hugged him anyway. They kissed and he said I need a hot bath and some clean pajamas. When he finished bathing and dressing, they both crawled into bed. It was dark outside and neither one was very hungry.

They lay in bed and Caroline said, "Philip, I have something to tell you."

Philip asked, "What's on your mind?"

She paused and was anxious to tell him the news. She said quietly, "I'm pregnant." Philip acted stunned, and took a long moment to respond. After a long pause he said, "You know, I thought you had been gaining some weight. I couldn't figure how you could gain weight with the sparse food we eat on the trail." Caroline looked somewhat shaken. Philip snuggled her and with a smile he said, "I was just joking sweetheart. I figured it out awhile back."

Caroline smiled at her lover and told him "I was pregnant before we left the ranch. I didn't want to tell you because I knew you would postpone leaving until the child was born. And then we would stay awhile before you would let us leave. Actually, I am pretty far along and may have to have our baby on the trip."

Philip said softly, "You are a strong, remarkable woman. Everything will be fine and I am so happy for us."

"As a final thing to say about it, we should make wagers as to the town we will be closest to when you have the child." They both laughed. Philip had a quick bath got into bed, and they kissed and hugged one another, and both went to sleep.

Chapter 34
Taking Care of Business, and Relaxing

The pioneers had finally reached LaGrange, Texas. The journey had been very slow and rugged. Even so, the folks were happy and excited. They had traveled about one quarter of the way to their destination.

They were all settled in their places to stay. Everyone was enjoying staying in a town. The next morning, Philip told Jake, "We need to visit the sheriff and tell him the story of the bandits."

Jake replied, "Let's go right now." The two walked down the wooden sidewalks and found the sheriff's office about a block away.

The two brothers knocked on the door and went inside. There was a big man sitting in a comfortable chair with his boots crossed on his desk. The gentleman spoke, "What can I do for you folks? My name is Robert McKetta. I go by Randy, but you can just call me Sheriff." He stood up and walked toward the men. Philip said, "I'm Philip Smith and this is my brother, Jake. We would like to make a report to you."

Philip continued, "We are on our way to Central Texas to settle some land. Two nights ago, we were camped at a nice spot. We were getting comfortable and two bandits charged into our camp and shot a couple of bullets into the air. They had stopped close to the campfire. One of the bandits then told us to "Drop all you guns on the ground. We are going to take some of your stuff. There will be no talking or I will kill one of you. Do you understand?"

"We did what they said. As they were rummaging through our wagons, little did they know that Jake was in the woods near the camp. Our three drovers were on the other side of the wagons tending to the cattle. The four men had heard the shots. The four of them had figured out what was going on. They silently closed in and surrounded the bandits. Without being heard or seen they had gotten the drop on the thieves. One of our cowboys said rather loudly, "Drop all your guns on the ground or I will drop them for you." They did so.

Philip said, "I walked to them, and pulled their bandanas off their faces, and picked up their weapons. I said loudly, "Everyone take a look, this is what cowards look like. I told the bandits to "Mount your horses and leave fast." That they did, especially when I slapped the rump of the first horse. Jake told the Sheriff "We are turning their weapons in to you now."

The story had gotten the Sheriff's attention. "Well, that is quite a story. Are all your folks all right?"

Jake replied, "Everyone is fine, thanks."

The Sheriff asked, "Can you give me a description of the two outlaws?"

Philip said, "Better than that, the one that didn't talk was about 5ft. 8 inches, and the talkative one was fairly tall, probably right at 6 feet. My brother, Jake, is an artist and he could probably make sketches of their faces if you have some paper and a pencil."

The Sheriff said, "Excellent!" He brought Jake the paper and pencil, and Jake quickly sketched the face of each bandit. The sketches were very recognizable. Sheriff McKetta picked up the drawings and looked at them intensely. He said, "I've seen these two in town. I will make these into wanted posters, and if they ever show up in my town again, they will be arrested on the spot. I want to thank you two so much, we shall serve justice if the chance arises. You are good citizens, Jake and Philip, and I hope you enjoy your stay in our little town."

Randy continued, "I will need for you to write down the date, approximate time, and exactly what happened. I would also need both of you please sign the document. When I sign and date the statement, it will be all I need to get the Judge to issue a warrant so that they can be arrested. Thank you again fellows, and have a great trip."

With the meeting completed, the brothers shook the Sheriff's hand, thanked him, and left the office. Jake told his brother as they were walking back to the hotel, "Maybe I need to become a lawman."

They both laughed and Philip said, "It will be hard enough to be a cattle rancher."

They returned to the hotel and met with Caroline and Julia. They decided together to ask the three cowboys to have dinner with the family. Jake immediately said, "I will ride to see them right now, and tell them to come to the hotel around 6 ." Jake tended to be a little impulsive at times. He was a man of action. He mounted his horse and rode off to see the vaqueros.

Jake got to Mr. Hodge's ranch in a flash. He saw Pedro, and rode up to him. He asked, "Donde esta Antonio?" Pedro ran to get Antonio and Jose. They hurried up to see Jake. Jake asked them "Would like to have dinner with us at the hotel around six o'clock? They all said "Si, senor, gracias." Jake turned on a dime, his horse reared up on his back hooves, and Jake took off like a bullet and shouted, "Hasta la vista Amigos!"

A little before 6, the cowboys walked into the hotel, dressed in clean clothes and with their hair combed. They went to the desk, and Krissie told them, "Mr. Smith told me you gentlemen will be having dinner with them, welcome. You may go to the bar and I will notify the Smiths that you are here. Mr. Philip told me that the drinks are on him." The guys went into the restaurant and the bar was on one end. Each ordered a beer and they were very relaxed.

About 5 minutes later, the Smith clan appeared in the restaurant. A server escorted them to a large reserved table. Jake saw the cowboys at the bar and waved them over to the table. Everyone was happy to see each other. The server, asked, "Welcome to the LaGrange Hotel, can I start you off with something to drink?"

Philip said, "We would like 5 beers, 1 glass of water, and a small glass of apple juice for Julia." The server said, "You've got it, I will bring the beverages and I can take your food order whenever you want. My name is Rosetta, but I go by Setta. She turned and headed to the bar.

At the table, Philip asked the guys, "How is your stay at the Hodges' place?" Antonio replied, "Everything is great. The bunks are comfortable, we have a tub for a hot bath, and the food is good. The cattle are just fine. Mr. Hodges has hay that we can feed to the herd."

Jake said, "That's great. It is quite a treat to have civilized living, even for a short while." Setta came back to the table and everyone ordered what they wanted to eat. Philip said, "We will need another round of drinks, same as before please Miss Setta."

Setta told them, "I will place the order immediately and you shall have your food soon."

"I know you will like your dinner. Richard Carroll is the best chef in this territory. He was a renowned chef and owned a small, busy restaurant in New York City. He sold the place and moved here because he wanted his own land. Oh, and by the way, after some time, we dated, and I am now Mrs. Carroll." Everyone smiled.

The folks were having fun and everyone was talking at one time. There were smiles on everyone's face. Caroline tapped her glass and they all got quiet. I have an announcement, "I am pregnant. I have been with child for the entire trip. Philip had figured it out, but I'm not sure all of you have yet."

"I will be riding Lightning for the remainder of the trip. Since we travel so slowly, it will be a much smoother ride than on the wagon. Those wooden wheels bounce me every time one hits even the smallest rock or branch. "I'm afraid that if we hit one more rock, I might have the baby on the spot." Everyone laughed. Caroline was a funny lady. She could always calm a nervous situation with humor.

Setta served them their orders and said, "Please let me know if you need anything. You are such a charming family." She turned, and went back to her station. The food was excellent and everyone cleaned their plate. When Setta returned, she brought the bill to Philip and asked, "Did you folks like the dinner?" All at the same time, everyone spoke about how wonderful the dinner was. The only distinct sound was Pedro saying, "Muy Bueno."

Krissie had left her desk for a short time. She had asked Setta if she could go to the table with her. Setta thought it to be a great idea. Krissie was right behind Setta and she had something behind her back. While Setta was giving the bill to Philip, Krissie kept walking and stopped at Julia's seat.

"Here is a special treat for a special young lady," Krissie proclaimed. With that, she brought her hand around and set down a piece of chocolate cake with chocolate icing. She then said, "This is on the house." Julia squealed with joy as the treat was presented to her.

Julia almost cried when she looked at Krissie, and said, "Thank you Krissie!" Her new friend leaned over gave her a kiss on the forehead, and quietly whispered to Julia, "You're welcome sweetheart."

The diners were all full of food from the excellent cuisine. Everybody seemed to be talking at the same time. Philip tapped his glass three times. They all got silent. He said, "I've got a proposition for you folks. This stop has been so recuperative, both physically and mentally. I would like to know if you would want to stay one more night. Then we could load up, and leave after a good breakfast here the day after tomorrow. If so, hold your right hand up if you are in."

Needless to say, everyone at the table raised their hands high. Julia silently continued to hold her hand in the air. Everyone else had lowered their hands and they all seemed so pleased. Philip saw Julia and asked her, "Julia, do you have a question?"

Julia asked, "What does 'recoopershun' mean? Jake took over here and said, "It means that both our bodies and minds are rested and strong. The word is recuperative." He added, "Sometimes I think Philip might have read too many books." Laughter erupted. All was well.

Philip spoke, "Well, we are all in agreement. Let's gather here at 8 o'clock for a hearty breakfast the day after tomorrow. We can sleep in or just be lazy for awhile tomorrow." After breakfast on the morning we will leave, we will prepare the next step of our journey. Everyone try to get a good night's sleep.

As the folks were walking up the stairs to retire to their rooms, Jake asked Philip "Do you remember what Dad said when we left?" Philip looked puzzled and couldn't really remember, since so many things had happened since they left. Jake told his brother that Dad had told us to check with the post office in LaGrange because he and Mom would try to mail a letter to us here. Philip was upset with himself because he rarely forgets anything.

Jake knew by the look on Philip's face that he was upset. Jake told his brother, "Look Philip, I barely remembered it myself, and don't take it so hard. After all, we have been through so many situations and you feel you have to be the one that makes sure everything is going right. Besides, you are the old man, and it happens," he said as a joke. Philip relaxed and said, "I am surely glad that you little rascal that you didn't forget."

Jake said, "Don't worry big brother, nothing will be told to the others and you and I can just go to the post office tomorrow before we leave" "Thanks Jake," Philip replied.

Chapter 35
On The Road Again

Everyone showed up at the hotel right at 8 on the second morning. They all ate a tasty and hardy breakfast. The whole group was very relaxed and raring to go. After they finished breakfast, each of the group knew what they needed to do.

Caroline and Julia went to the general store to buy provisions for the next leg of the trip. When they entered the store, a young lady greeted the two with, "Welcome to our store. My name is Rhonda, and if there is anything you need, please ask."

"Nice to meet you Rhonda," said Caroline. We will need food, ammunition, two blankets and two dresses for me, as my shape is changing with the child that I am bearing." Caroline felt like she needed to buy something for Julia. She decided to buy enough fabric so that she could make matching dresses for Julia and Dolly when they finally made it to their new home. Rhonda said, "I will help you find everything you want."

They gathered the sundries and then looked at the fabric and ladies dresses. Rhonda showed Caroline some dresses that might fit her better at this time. Both the dresses she showed her were adjustable. Caroline chose the two simple long dresses and tried them on. They fit comfortably and were reasonably priced.

Next, Rhonda took them to the fabric bolts to pick cloth for the dresses for Julia and Dolly. Caroline let Julia decide on the fabric. She chose a beautiful sky blue cloth with a floral print. Julia was ecstatic and full of joy. She said to her mom, "Thank you mother I am so happy." Caroline told her as she was hugging her princess, "We will make the dresses soon after we settle in our new home. I can teach you how to sew when we make Dolly's dress. We can work on that at the campfire and make your dress when we are settled."

Jake and Philip had left quickly after breakfast and walked to the post office. When they arrived, there was a letter for the folks from Jacob and Elizabeth. Philip told Jake, "We can pull this out and read it at the campfire tonight." Jake nodded and grinned.

Philip, Jake, and the vaqueros were in the street and they all mounted their horses and rode out to the Hodges' ranch. When the men reached the ranch, the brothers hitched up the wagons. They got the horses and tied them behind the wagons.

The cowboys rode to the corral and geared up their horses. They loaded the tents, sleeping bags, and everything else they would need. Then they rode over to the cattle. They would wait there until everyone was ready to go.

Philip and Jake walked to Mr. Hodges' front door and knocked. Daniel answered the door with a smile and said, "Looks like you folks are ready to leave soon. And by the way, this is my lovely wife Dianna." They exchanged greetings as they shook her hand.

Philip told him, "Yes Sir, we are all ready to keep moving. We really appreciate you letting us stay and taking care of the animals. Here is the amount we agreed upon." Jake gave Mr. Hodges the gold coins in the amount specified. Jake and Philip shook hands with Daniel Hodges and thanked him again for his hospitality.

The brothers drove the wagons to the corral. Jake asked Antonio, "Listos Senores?" Jake had been learning Spanish mostly because he liked the idea of speaking in a different language. Antonio replied, "Si, Jefe."

Philip asked them to "Please stay with the cattle, and Jake and I will go back to town to pick up Caroline, Julia, and the provisions."

The brothers went back to town and stopped at the general store. They got any other provisions that they figured they would need. They then went to the hotel and to pick the girls up.

The girls helped the men load and pack the supplies that they had bought. Jake helped Julia climb up on the wagon. Philip helped Caroline mount Lightning. They headed back to the Hodges' ranch and the cowboys had the cattle ready to move. They finished with their organized packing, and made sure that all of the wagon train was totally ready to go.

They were loaded up and they headed out to leave the ranch. Mr. and Mrs. Hodges were at his door, and they waved at the travelers. All of the travelers waved back. They exited his ranch through the gate and the caravan turned right on the primitive road heading northwest. The next time they would see civilization, it would be the town of Bastrop. All was good.

They started down a rudimentary road which was pretty good for a couple of miles. After that, the road was barely discernible, and they were on the prairie again. They reverted back to the campfire way, and yet they were all so invigorated with the rest, baths, beds, and well cooked food, that they had a renewed spirit.

They found a good spot to camp near a small lake. After the folks made the campfire and ate some dinner, Philip and Jake, the brothers made their way to the campfire. Philip pulled an envelope from his pocket. Philip said, "Jake and I picked up this letter from Matagorda. Everyone got excited and knew

who it must be from. Philip read the address on the envelope
and it read: **To the Smith Family and Friends**
        General Delivery
        LaGrange, Texas

Jake opened the letter and it said, *"Dear Ones, Elizabeth and I
hope that all is well with you folks. You must be well on your way to
your new land. We are doing well and the ranching business is
doing well also. We love you all and miss you so already. We pray
for you every day and hope you are having the time of your lives.
Send us a letter if you can sometime and we know you are happy.
We send all our love, Grandpa and Grandma. Give a kiss for Julia."*

Chapter 36
What a Wonderful World

After several days and nights of traveling, Jake yelled out, "Now would you look at that!" What Jake was pointing to in the far off distance was a giant pine forest. Philip, the reader and path maker, knew that this existed. He calmly said, "What you are now seeing is known as 'The Lost Pines' of Bastrop." The only one to ever see something like this was Philip when he was a child in Germany.

Philip continued "There are conifer forests in East Texas, and a few in far West Texas. But here sits a beautiful evergreen forest. Most of what we've seen of Texas was sparse trees, scrub brush, and lovely grass that cover the prairies. We have also have seen some spectacular old Live Oak Trees. Some of those trees were hundreds of years old and had canopies that could cover an area as large as a city block in Galveston."

"Somewhere in that forest is a town named Bastrop that we will find. When we leave Bastrop, we will have to ford the Colorado River. We will inquire when we are in town, both the best spot to cross the great river, as well as the best way to continue to Round Rock, Texas."

It appeared to the travelers that they were a day or two away from the forest. Everyone was awed as they got closer to such a magnificent sight. They camped one more night before reaching Bastrop. The travelers all were in great spirits knowing they were close to civilization again.

They made camp and took care of the animals as well as themselves. It was one of their favorite camping spots of the whole trip. The closer they got to a town, the more important it was to have security. Therefore, they reinstated the night-watch schedule. None of them wanted to have an incident like they had before. All things went well that night knowing that there was a constant watch.

Chapter 37
Civilization Again

The sun rose the next morning and revealed one of the most beautiful sunrises any of them had ever seen. Everyone was very excited and they packed up the wagons, gathered the cattle and tied the horses behind the wagons. They started out for Bastrop with excitement and joy. They stayed glued to the view of the approaching forest. The closer they got, the more intense the feelings became.

When they were close to the town, they were once again on a rudimentary road, which with each mile got better due to workers attending to the road condition near the town. It was almost glorious as they made it to the city limits of Bastrop. Not only would the settlers be able to have the creature comforts that were non-existent in the wilderness, but to be in such a wonderful sense of being in a town that was surrounded by a forest.

Their eyes were big and their hearts were beating just a bit faster than usual as they rode down the main street of Bastrop. They stopped at the small hotel in the middle of town. The cowboys rounded up the cattle, waiting for the orders of what they would be doing next. Just like in LaGrange, Philip and Jake went inside the hotel.

Bastrop was a smaller town than LaGrange, and there was only one hotel. The hotel was clean and nice. It had no restaurant, but there was a nice one next door. The hotel had a sign above the door stating "The Pine Tree Hotel." The setting, however, was enchanting. The brothers got down, and went in to the hotel and approached the reception desk inside.

Philip asked the desk clerk, "Is there a spot nearby where we could corral our cattle, as well as our wagons, horses and oxen?"

The clerk, whose name was Dinah, asked him, "How many head of cattle do you have?"

Jake replied, "We have 20 head." Dinah told them of a small farm outside the town, where they could put them up. It's the second place on the left as you leave town. The owner is Neal Leavell and his wife, Cherie.

The family checked in, and Philip had told the cowboys to drive the cattle to the Leavell's place. They had already gotten two hotel rooms. Philip and Jake had unloaded what they needed and took their gear to the rooms. The brothers helped Caroline and Julia dismount and went inside and took them to their room. As it was in LaGrange, the cowboys had a place to stay, bathe, and eat at the Leavell's place.

The men drove the cattle to the ranch. The brothers had driven the wagons out with the herd. They arrived and talked to Neal Leavell, the owner of the small ranch. Neal greeted them warmly and showed them where everything was. The cowboys got settled in, and Jake and Philip returned to the "Pine Tree." Before they left, Philip again asked the cowboys if they would join the family at the restaurant around 6 for dinner. Antonio said, "Gracias, Jefe".

The cowboys were all settled and bathed, and they met the family at the café a little before six. Caroline was very pregnant, and Philip had arranged for them to stay in a downstairs room. The whole gang met, had a great dinner, and all went to their rooms for the night. The vaqueros rode back to the Leavell Ranch.

During dinner there was a conversation around the dinner table. The discussion was about how long to stay in Bastrop. They all finally agreed that they would just stay one night.

The general point being made was that they were ready to keep moving, and get to "The Promised Land." Jake said, "O.K. folks, we will eat breakfast in the morning, go pick up our cattle and keep on moving. Philip and I will get the wagons ready, and we'll come get the girls, and then go meet with the herd on the way out of town."

The next morning, they ate, then went to the Leavell Ranch and got the whole group together. They started out once again. Caroline had been riding Lightning for the last several days. The wooden wheels, and poor suspension, made for a bumpy ride on the wagon. They continued on their journey. As was with every other town, there was a decent road out of town. The roads looked and felt less like a road with each mile they traveled away from the towns.

They went a few miles and it started to get dark. They found a nice place under some big trees near a small creek. They pitched their tents and tended to the animals. No one would admit it, but they were already getting fairly tired of the daily ordeal. Philip sensed what they felt, and at the campfire that night he said, "Listen up folks. We are all getting weary with our travels. But, we knew what we were getting into before we started."

"I just want to say that all of you are the bravest people I have ever known. And you know that I have even seen war. No one has complained, and each of you has done more that your share of the work. Here we are in the middle of nowhere, happy, yet weary. I wouldn't have wanted to be with anyone else on earth than you folks.

We are more than halfway to our goal, and it probably won't get easier. We simply need to persist, smile, and keep our dreams in our heads." All of the folks around the fire smiled and nodded at what Philip had said. There would never be one complaint about anything the rest of the way.

When they went to their tent, Philip, Caroline and Julia all snuggled together. There was peace and endearing love among the family. Nobody said a word and they all fell into a deep sleep. They slept all night and woke up with the sun, rejuvenated.

The group had stayed in the part of Bastrop that was on the southern side of the Colorado River. A kind gentleman in town had suggested a place where the crossing would be the easiest. It was in a bend in the river about 5 miles northwest of town. This was the place they chose to camp. Tomorrow, they would take on the might of the famous Colorado River.

Chapter 38
"Troublemaker"

They awoke early the next morning. Philip said to the folks, "This will be a day we'll never forget!" They had all prepared for this undertaking. The place in the river was not deep, except in spots. The men would first drive the cattle across the river. They proceeded to drive the cattle with meticulous skill. The cowboys and the Smith brothers carefully, but intensely, herded the cattle across the river.

It was a flat bank into the river and they successfully got most of the animals across. They forced them to walk across the shallows, and really encouraged them to swim in two spots. They made it across with all the stock except for one very young bull calf. The men were across the river on their horses, and Jake was near the bank. The calf was across the river but had strayed too close to the bank. Philip saw something and shouted out, "Jake! The calf has fallen into the river!"

Jake saw the animal that was struggling mightily. Jake jumped off his horse and dived into the river. He grabbed the calf, and pulled him across a current. He was lucky that a broken log was sweeping right at him and the calf. Jake grabbed the log while holding on to the calf's neck. Philip yelled, "Hold on tight Jake, I'm on my way."

Philip took off on Lightning at a fast pace. He had an idea. Philip rode the horse downstream past where Jake and the calf were. He hopped off his steed, and tied a rope to the saddle horn. He ran to the river bank ahead of Jake with his rope rolled up. He had converted the end into a lasso. Philip was a skilled cowboy. Jake, the calf, and the log were coming close to the bank where Philip was. He swung the rope in a circular motion over his head. Philip then tossed the rope and landed the loop over a large branch of the log.

He pulled back on the rope, and tightened the loop around the branch. By that time, Antonio and Pedro were right beside Philip. Jose was with Lightning and he was backing the horse up slowly until the rope was tight. The others grabbed the taut rope and began to pull their prize in slowly, yet surely. Jake and the calf were fighting both the current and the weight. The men on the bank slowly brought the log to through the current toward the river bank. Remarkably, they pulled Jake and the calf to the shallow bank.

Philip and the two vaqueros jumped into the shallow water. Philip had grabbed the log and untied the rope. Jake and the other two grabbed the calf and pulled him up on the bank. Philip retrieved his rope just as the log was swept away in a strong current. Jake and the calf climbed up the bank and were safely out of the river. All four of the men were on solid ground, as was the young calf.

Jake said, "Good job boys. I will always remember this calf until he grows into a powerful bull. When he's grown, I will personally ride that critter. He will, from now on, be known as 'Troublemaker'." The men laughed, and fell down on the ground from exhaustion as they watched "Troublemaker" run to his mama. He latched on to one of her teats and held on for dear life.

Jake said to no one special, "Yes sir, when Troublemaker is the biggest, strongest bull of the herd, I will climb on his back and ride him like the vaquero rodeo cowboys do in Mexico."

Philip replied, "That will be something that I sure do look forward to seeing." All the men laughed again, especially Jake.

With the calf safe, Philip said, "Okay boys, the fun part is over. We now need to get the wagons, people and oxen over this river. The men left their horses tied to trees and went upstream and dove into the river. They swam across and came out close to where the wagons were.

Chapter 39
Let's Do This Thing

Caroline and Julia were standing by the wagons. The men got back across the river without a glitch. Caroline was really showing her pregnancy, and it appeared that the child would be born sometime soon. The plan was to take the wagons up stream. Four men each would take a corner and gently urge the oxen to cross with the wagon. They had to swim at one place in the river and the guys held on and kicked and swam the wagon through the deep water. The wagons were made of wood, and the brothers had previously sealed the bottom of the wagons. The first wagon reached the shore and the oxen pulled it out of the river. Then they jumped in and swam back across to help get the second wagon across.

Philip pulled Caroline away from the others. "Caroline, my dear one," Philip said, "We have two options to get you to the other side of the river. You can ride in the second wagon when we swim them over, or, you can swim with us when we go. Do you think you are up to it?"

Caroline replied, "Philip, you know that I am an excellent swimmer. I can make it across, even with my extra weight." Philip then told her, "I will hold your arm and we will swim the river together."

Caroline replied, "So shall it be."

The next step was for all the men to roll the second wagon into the river, and swim it across. They were ready to take the second wagon the same way they did with the first. Then the final goal was to have everyone who was left on the other side swim across.

Philip said, "I will have Jake hold on to Julia when they swim across."

Philip was with Caroline, and Jake was with Julia. They slowly entered the water, and began swimming across. Philip had a strong grip of Caroline's arm on the farthest part of her arm up toward her shoulder. Jake had Julia get on his back as high as she could and put her arms around Jake's neck. None of them showed fear, and within a very few minutes, everyone was climbing up the opposite river bank in good shape.

The Colorado River in Central Texas

Chapter 40
Get Some Rest

They finally got everything back together and the cattle were settled with the trusty cowboys tending to them. All the tents were pitched and the evening campfire was calming. Everyone had agreed that they would make camp that night near the edge of the Colorado River. Jake said, "Would you take a look at that sunset!" to no one in particular.

It was one of those magnificent Texas sunsets that happens every so often. It occurs when there are layers of stratus clouds in the west. The colors were interspersed with orange, yellow, red and pink on the palate of the sky, which was so blue that you could feel it.

Everyone sat around the fire as it was getting dark. They had cooked up a couple of rabbits that Jose had shot and prepared. It was a fine, wilderness meal along with some dry beans that had been cooking for awhile. They also had some hard biscuits that Caroline had made a couple of days ago.

It was a magic time around the campfire. They were all eating and feeling pretty darn good. The settlers were exhausted, yet, amazingly energetic. The day had been the toughest one they ever had on the trail, and they conquered everything that had been thrown at them.

Each person spoke as they told their version of the river crossing. Philip, who had been unusually quiet, spoke up. He said, "I really wasn't sure that we could pull that little stunt off. But when we got started, and I had looked around at everyone, and my heart and mind knew that we were going to get this done. I am so proud of you all. Together, we are amazing, and I know we can handle anything that comes up."

They all nodded agreement, and each felt particularly proud for a job well done. Jake spoke and said, "How about that little girl and her pregnant momma swimming across that river?" There were cheers and clapping. Julia stood up and took a bow. The guys all stood and gave the little cutie a standing ovation. Caroline spoke next and said, "When the four of you guys saved that calf and showed your skills, I was quite impressed, very well done!"

Julia spoke up next, "I liked the part when Troublemaker ran straight to his mommy, and latched on to a teat to calm down and have some breakfast." They all laughed at the way Julia had told her story. She had used hand gestures to represent the calf and the mother as she told her story.

The travelers all felt both pride and fatigue. It wasn't long before everyone was sleeping deeply, except for the watcher on duty. The next morning, they stoked the fire, and made coffee and some pancakes. They all had confidence as the caravan took off once again. This time they were headed to Round Rock, Texas. In Bastrop, they had purchased more than enough supplies and food for the remainder of the journey.

The group proceeded northwest towards Round Rock. This part of the journey went very smoothly, and the camping and other mundane necessities had become habit. The folks traveled slowly, and had been on the path for a couple of weeks.

During a campfire a few days later, Caroline told everyone around the circle, "Folks, the baby will be born soon." Jake had a look on his face that showed that he had never heard those words before. Everyone seemed to be so happy for Caroline and Philip, especially big sister, Julia.

Chapter 41
Still a Long Way to Go

The travelers all got a great night's sleep. They would still continue their watch after the episode with the bandits, however. They all started waking as the sun came up. Everyone did their duty to make sure that everything was ready to go. The group had it down and the whole band was like a fine tuned guitar. They loaded up and got the cattle bunched up, and they were on the way again.

The settlers had traveled more than half way to their destination. They continued on a northwestern trek. There had been some small communities, but the next town of any size was Round Rock. They were now traveling on prairie land which had dark, soft soil. Philip said to his brother, "This is mighty fine farmland if one was of such a mind."

Jake replied, "Yes sir, but our minds are meant to be on becoming Texas cattle ranchers." That was what their minds were really focused on.

The caravan was moving very slowly, as it always had done. Caroline rode Lightning parallel with Philip as he drove the wagon. She was much more comfortable on horseback than on the bumpy wagon. Philip caught a glimpse of her with his peripheral vision, and turned his head to her. He asked, "How are you doing?"

She replied, "You know I am tough and am doing well, but, you need to know that I am getting close to childbirth."

Philip asked her, "What do you want to do?" "We can turn back to Bastrop or veer to a different route and go to Austin." Caroline slowed her steed down to a stop. Philip did the same with his wagon. He said, "Let's get down and have an easy walk. It will probably clear both our minds."

Philip helped her off the horse and the two got down to the flat ground. Philip tied Lightning to the wagon. He took Caroline's hand and they slowly walked as they were talking. Philip asked, "How are you really doing?"

She replied, "Philip, I'm a little scared about having a baby in the wilderness. I am used to being in a bed where there is someone who knows about birthing a baby."

Philip told her, "You just say the word and we will head straight for a place with a bed."

Caroline looked deeply into his eyes and told him, "You know me, Philip, more than anyone else on earth. I am as tough as I need to be. You have been with me for two deliveries, and you guys can make something as comfortable as any bed. I can drink fresh milk from the cows. We always have at least one with milk, and the boys can provide meat from hunting game.

When the time comes, I will tell you, and we will find a place under a giant live oak tree by a creek with clear, pure water. We have been through this and we know what to do. I love you and am ready for whatever comes."

Philip drew his face close to hers, and gazed deep into her soul. He said, "No man can love a woman any more than I do right now." They kissed for the longest time. With no more words, they walked back to the wagon. He helped her up to the wagon step, then on to Lightning. She had started riding side saddle to avoid any possible problems with the baby. Philip stepped up to the driver's bench and got settled, and the caravan started up again.

The group continued as they had done before. They traveled until the sun was about to set, and set up their camp as they always had done. At the campfire, they talked about the day before and the river crossing. Jake said, "You know something folks, people might forget many things in their lives, but they remember things that stand out. I don't think any of us will ever forget crossing the Colorado River." Everyone except Jake clapped their approval. The travelers went to bed early that night and they all slept hard.

Chapter 42
We Need a Little Break

They all got up the next morning, had a scant breakfast, and broke camp to continue the journey. They had gone a short distance and Caroline stopped her horse. She got down and sat on the ground. Philip realized that something wasn't right. He turned the wagon around in a circle and drove to where Caroline was. Trying not to seem anxious, he asked her, "Caroline, is there anything wrong?"

She answered quietly, "Philip, I believe I will have this baby very soon."

It was in early August, 1854, and very hot. Caroline told everyone around the campfire that night, "I will be having this baby anytime now." Philip, Jake and Julia moved toward Caroline and gave her a big hug. Philip spoke to the group, "Well folks, it looks like we will arrive a little later than we thought before. We will set a temporary camp which will protect us and stay until Caroline has the baby. We will wait until Caroline and the baby are strong enough to proceed."

"I have been with her through two child births, and I am pretty sure that I know what I need to do," Philip said. Antonio stood up and said, "I have delivered three children in Monterey, and surely together, we should have it handled." Caroline spoke up and said, "Well I am so glad that I have two experienced gentlemen to assist me, but I will have to do most of the work myself. Thank you guys for being with me and helping."

The group parked the wagons under a giant live oak tree for shade and limiting the light rain that had started falling.

They unloaded one wagon, and found as many quilts, blankets and other soft material to make a bed for Caroline. After that, they pulled the cover over the wagon and set it tight so that no rainwater could get in.

The men then made a makeshift corral for the cattle. Everyone pitched their tents, and secured the other animals. They had set up a pretty comfy little squatters' village. They were well ready for an extended stay. There was a running creek very close to their camp.

Philip whistled to the others and gestured for them to come. When they got close enough, Philip said, "Let's help her into the wagon and get everything battened down." He told the group, "We may be here for awhile."

They all brought back whatever they could find and cleared out the floor of the wagon, and made a bed for Caroline. They helped her into the wagon and she settled on the bed. Philip gathered them all and said, "We will be staying here until Caroline has her child and the two of them are strong enough to continue the journey. So, pitch your tents and find some firewood.

That night, Philip brought Caroline food, and he ate with her. She was still able to get around, if needed. Antonio had put the wagon tail gate down to horizontal, and put a box that went about half way up to the gate from the ground. Caroline was able to get in and out of the wagon with Philip's help. Caroline moved around on her new bed because she was uncomfortable. Julia stayed in the wagon with her mother. She was very concerned about her mom. She fell asleep early and slept all night long.

Chapter 43
A Child is Born

The next morning, Caroline and Philip woke up together. He had slept with her on the bed to comfort her. He looked at her with love and asked, "How are you doing?"

Caroline replied, "You know me, so far, I've had short labors and easy births. I'm not scared, I'm just sorry that I've had to stop the journey."

Philip stated, "No one in this band of brothers will have any ill feelings due to you having a child. They all love you, just not quite as much as I do. Besides, Antonio has delivered three children of his own, and he will help us when the time comes."After a few hours, Caroline called out for Philip, who was helping get the camping order and gathering firewood for the night. Philip appeared and asked, "Is there anything wrong?"

Caroline said with a funny little grin, "Nothing is wrong, I am ready to have a baby." Philip squeezed her hand and gave her a kiss and said, "Here we go." Together, they held hands and Philip gave a short prayer for the childbirth.

She was right about having short labors. Her contractions started about an hour after their conversation. Philip whistled and waved to Antonio who waved back in response. In a matter of a minute, Antonio was at the wagon. He tied his horse to the wagon and got his saddle bags. He asked Caroline, "Miss Caroline, do you mind if I help Philip?"

Caroline replied, "Philip told me you have delivered three babies for your wife. I am just pleased that I have a couple of fellas that know what they are doing. It's not personal, it's necessary for this to go well."

About 30 minutes later, Caroline said, "The baby is coming." Jake had whittled a smooth round stick that she could bite down on if the pain got to be too much. Julia was standing next to the wagon. Philip called Jake over and told him, "Hey brother, would you like to take Julia fishing until this is over. She will be able to come see her brother or sister when he or she gets here." Jake lifted her and told Julia, "Oh boy, we're going fishing." Off they went.

The birthing began. As Caroline had said, it only lasted for a very short time. The men saw the little head coming out, and they gently helped the baby out. Antonio had sharpened his knife and sterilized it over the open flame. When the baby was out, he cut the cord as he had done before. Everything went famously, and the child was wrapped and was in Philip's arms.

Philip waved everyone to the wagon. When they were close, he shouted out, "It's a boy!" Now our family has a beautiful, wonderful girl, and a baby boy that will someday become a cattle rancher." Caroline had made no noise during the process, although at times it looked like the veins in her neck might pop out of her skin.

After a few minutes, she sat up and ordered Philip, "O.K. darling husband, I need to hold our new baby." Philip gently handed the infant to his wife and the baby stopped crying. Philip got into the wagon and sat by his family. They had allowed Julia to crawl into the wagon and hold the baby. She would be part of many live births as she grew up on the ranch. She held the tiny person, and she was a natural. The baby made a cooing sound as Julia gently rocked the infant.

The baby was very comfortable, and Julia said with pride and a big smile, "I have a baby brother." Everyone had circled the wagon and they were congratulating the parents, and prattling with joyful words. Jake climbed into the wagon and said, "Please bow your heads. 'Heavenly Father, please bless this child and his family,' Amen."

Things settled down, and the folks went back to either their chores or whatever they wanted to do. They all realized that this would be their home for at least some time. Philip noticed a card game starting up and he smiled. Caroline asked Philip about the name since it was a boy. They had brought up possible names before, but the one that seemed to show up the most was 'Albert'. Philip said, "How about 'Charles Albert Smith'?" Caroline perked up as she said, "How thoughtful, as you know, Charles was my grandfather's name, and we both like 'Albert'."

Once again, Philip whistled and waved everyone to come near the wagon. When they were all assembled, Philip told them, "We have named the little guy 'Charles Albert Smith'." Wild clapping and whooping erupted, and there was joy in the air. Philip said, "Sorry to interrupt your game fellows." There was some fake jeering, which made Philip chuckle. "We will call him Albert. So when you talk to him, you can address him by his name."

"I want to once more say how happy and pleased we are to be honored with such wonderful folks. As our adventure continues, there most certainly will be more obstacles we must conquer. There will be many more joyous times as well. Thank you all for being our family." Everyone clapped and whooped again loudly. There was coherence and underlying trust throughout the entire troop.

Days came and went, and everything was quiet and even sometimes boring while waiting to get back on the trail. The vaqueros and Jake would take the cattle to different areas where the grass was tall and sweet to graze. One could tell that they were fattening up since they didn't have to walk every day, and they were able to eat lots of fresh healthy grass.

Meanwhile, Jake (the artistic one), had drawn a pencil sketch of Albert in Caroline's arms. He would hide it, and give it to her when they reached the ranch. He also was working on a cradleboard. A cradleboard is what the Native American women used to carry their babies. It is often incorrectly called a papoose. A papoose actually means 'baby' in some Native American languages. (6)

Jose had shot a deer a few days ago and they had skinned the animal. Jake treated the skin until it was soft. He worked to build the frame and shoulder harness. He cut the skin, and formed it into a cradle, or holder of the baby. That allowed the mother to carry the baby easily when walking, or on horseback.

He finished the cradleboard and surprised Philip and especially Caroline, one evening before dinner. They were both amazed and thankful. "This will be a big help," Caroline stated. Some Native American cradleboards were very ornate, but Jake had only the basic materials to create a workable cradleboard for Caroline. After a few days, Caroline asked Jake, "Jake, would you do the honor of putting the cradleboard on my back and placing Albert in it? I want to walk to where Philip is sitting and surprise him."

Jake replied, "I would be honored to do that. Are you sure you are strong enough to do this?"

Caroline gave him a stare that meant, "Are you kidding me?"

Jake smiled, and said, "You are probably strong enough to pull one of those wagons." They both chuckled, and Jake carefully secured the board on her back, and gently put the baby into the deer skin and strapped him in.

When everything was situated, Caroline and Jake walked quietly and carefully over to where Philip was sitting. He was talking and he didn't see them approach. When they were right next to him, he could see that his buddies were staring at something right behind him. He stood up quickly and turned around.

He couldn't believe what he was seeing. Caroline said quietly, "Good evening Philip."

Caroline asked Jake, "Would you mind taking Albert to his father?" Jake took the baby from the cradleboard and put him in his father's arms. Then he carefully took the cradleboard off of Caroline and set it down gently.

Jake told her, as you get used to it, you will be able to put it on and off by yourself. You probably will still need someone to help with Albert each time for awhile. But just look around, there are a lot of able bodied men who would be very happy to do that."

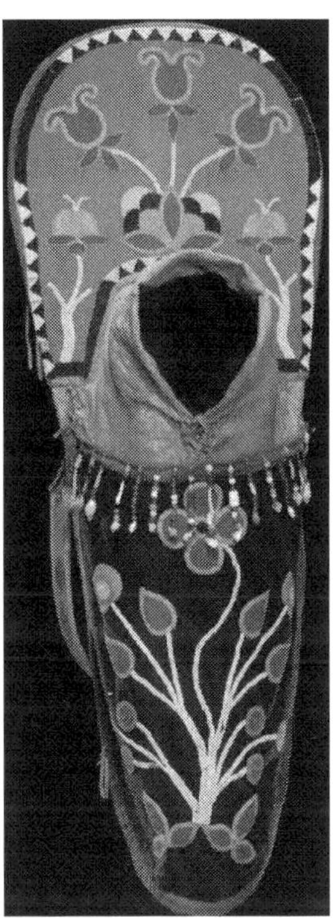

Ceremonial Cradleboard

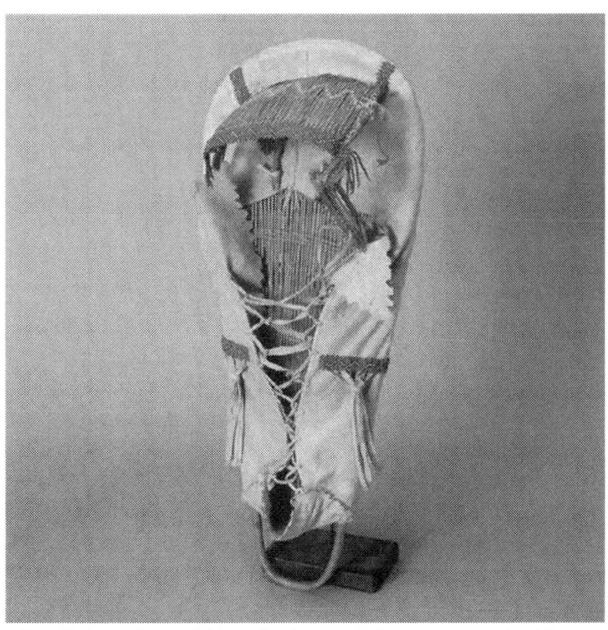

Jake's Cradleboard would be similar to this one except without the beads

Chapter 44
Respite

The group had been at their camp now for a few days. Caroline and Albert were both healthy and hungry. They were both getting stronger by the day. Julia stayed with her mom and little brother constantly.

Everyone was at peace and relaxing. It was the first time that Pedro had pulled his small guitar from the wagon. He played and sang Mexican popular songs. Jake borrowed the guitar one night and sang "She'll be Coming Round the Mountain When she Comes," in English with a German accent. The music and singing brought peace to the camp.

The break in their travel actually was a great blessing in so many different ways. A child was born and he was healthy. He also had ten fingers and ten toes. The other blessing was that both the humans and animals were well rested and had been eating well.

Chapter 45
Onward We Go

They had been at their camp now for eight days. Caroline and Albert were both doing very well. They were both getting stronger. Often, Caroline would let Julia rock him to sleep. The boys, on the other hand were enjoying the break quite a bit. They fished, hunted, played cards and took the herd to new places to graze. Everyone was at peace and relaxing.

Seven days after Albert was born, Caroline told Philip, "I think I am ready to travel again." This was the eighth day since they stopped.

Philip questioned her, "I know you are strong, but don't you think we need to wait a little bit longer?"

She said, "I feel like I could go now, but each day we do get stronger and stronger. Albert has a great appetite, and I can breast feed him until we get to the ranch."

Philip asked, "How about two more days? That will be a Sunday, and that seems appropriate."

She said, "That sounds good, we will be up to it."

Philip told the others that "We will be leaving in two days, so be ready."

The next day, the men worked on getting everything prepared to head out the following day. The stop actually had been a blessing in that everyone involved finally got the rest they needed.

Sunday came, and they took their tents down, and everything was packed. After breakfast, the vaqueros gathered the cattle, and Philip and Jake helped Caroline into the saddle on Lightning. Jake had correctly strapped the cradleboard on her back.

Jake jumped on Lightning behind the saddle, and Philip lifted Albert up to Jake. Jake then inserted Albert into the cradleboard and tightened the harness. It seemed to work perfectly. Jake asked Caroline, "How does everything feel with that thing on your back?"

She said, "Amazingly, it is very comfortable." With those words, Jake slipped off of Lightning and headed to the wagon.

The caravan was on the way again. They went extra slowly and made sure that they would find flat land without rocks so that it would be a smoother ride. The journey proceeded onward.

Chapter 46
Round Rock, Texas

They saw the town of Round Rock in the distance. Philip drove his wagon alongside Lightning and asked Caroline, "How are you doing sweetheart?"

She replied, "Albert and I feel great. This cradleboard seems to be helping me with my posture." They both laughed out loud. Philip said, "Very soon we will be sleeping on a bed, and we can check with a doctor or mid-wife to make sure everything is well."

They drove into town. It was the smallest town they had been to. They pretty much did the same things they had done in the other towns. There was a little hotel on Main Street, and they stopped in front of it. Jake was on the ground and took Albert out of the cradleboard and he handed Albert to Philip. Next, Jake helped Caroline off the horse, and the two brothers went into the hotel after Philip handed the baby back to his momma.

The boys went to the reception desk. A pretty, young lady asked, "What can I do for you folks? My name is Rachael, and I am the daughter of the owner, George Randolf."

Philip told her, "We will need 2 rooms, both rooms downstairs if possible. We will probably stay two nights. Also, we have a small herd of cattle. Is there a place close by where we can board the cowboys and corral the animals?"

Rachael said, "Yes, a man named John Walton has a small spread about ½ mile outside of town on the right. He is very nice and reasonable. Here are your room keys, and I need you to sign in please. Oh, and I forgot, my dad is out of town right now, but my mother, Silvia, is here and she will be available if you need her. She is the school teacher for the town during the day. She is very sweet and loves this hotel. I also help her teach when I do not have a day shift at the hotel.

Jake said, "We are brothers. I am Jake and this is my brother, Philip. We also have a two week old infant. Caroline, Philip's wife, had a child in the middle of nowhere. The couple also has a darling 4 year old daughter named Julia." Philip also asked Rachael, "Is there a doctor or mid-wife in town that could check out Caroline and the baby Albert?"

Rachael replied, "There is a Dr. Weber, who has a clinic right down the street. He and his wife, Yvonne, live in the back, but he is almost always there. He is very kind and is a wonderful doctor."

Jake got the room keys and went and opened one of the rooms. He and Philip went outside and escorted Julia and Caroline in, holding little Albert. When they walked by the desk, Rachael got so excited, and asked Caroline, "Would it be rude if I asked you to hold Albert for a second?"

Caroline walked around the desk and placed Albert in Rachael's arms. Rachel carefully cuddled him, and sang him a sweet song. Albert loved her, and she loved him instantly. She gently gave the baby back to Caroline and said, "Thank you, what a sweet child.

Everything was good. The family had two rooms, and the vaqueros were bunking at the Walton ranch near the cattle. The folks went into their hotel rooms. Everyone was exhausted. They all went into the rooms and everyone got into bed, and immediately fell asleep, except Caroline. She had to feed baby Albert. When she was finished, she placed the baby next to his sleeping father in the bed. Caroline crawled into bed on the other side of Albert, and she fell asleep as well.

They had arranged with the cowboys to meet for dinner at 6 P.M. at a café near the hotel called 'The Monument'. The three amigos had cleaned up and were sitting in the café when the Smiths came in shortly thereafter. They all felt really good and hungry. Jake asked around to find out what folks liked the most at this café. The majority told them that the steak was juicy and delicious. Jake felt like he had to tell the folks the result of his poll.

They all ordered steak with salad except Julia. She was having pan-fried chicken, potatoes, and milk. During the dinner, there were many conversations. The group talked about the journey so far. They had made it most of the way to the ranch, and they only had around 55 miles left to reach their new home.

Philip spoke up and said, "I would like to just stay one night here so that we can get on our way. We can get provisions tomorrow and head out in the morning." They all nodded their agreement and each one knew their responsibilities.

After dinner, Philip and Caroline took Albert and walked to Dr. Weber's office. They knocked on the door and found a tall, friendly man. He opened the door and invited them in. "My name is Lew Weber. My wife and I live in the back of the house. Wait just a minute and can meet my wife." Dr. Weber went to the back and returned with a lovely woman on his arm. Lew said, "This is my wife for many years. I present you my sweetheart forever, Yvonne."

Mrs. Weber said to the visitors, "I am so glad to meet you."

Philip replied, "We are very pleased to meet you both. You seem like such happy people. I am Philip Smith, and this is my precious wife, Caroline, and our newborn son, Albert. We were hoping that you could check out the mother and baby. She gave birth to the baby while we were on the trail. It seems like they are both doing well, but we just wanted a doctor to examine them both in case there might be something wrong."

Dr. Weber said, "Philip, you take a seat here and I will examine them in my office." Philip sat down as Yvonne retired to the back room. The doctor took the mother and son into the examining room. After just a few minutes they came back into the waiting room.

Dr. Weber stated, "They are both in excellent health. Make sure that Caroline gets some protein, such as beef, deer or rabbit when you can. She is nursing very well. At this stage, and the circumstances involved, I'd say these nice people should have no problems." Philip and Caroline thanked him, paid him for his services and left his house.

The next morning, everyone had breakfast at The Monument Café. They all knew the drill. The vaqueros and the brothers would go by horseback to the Walton ranch. When they arrived, the cowboys would round up the cattle and wait. Philip and Jake would tie their horses to the back of the wagons, and they would drive the wagons into town.

When they reached the hotel, Jake helped Julia onto his wagon. Caroline had decided that she was still more comfortable riding Lightning with Albert in the cradleboard instead of on a wagon. Philip was right by the horse to help Caroline mount the steed and he also placed and secured Albert in the cradleboard. Philip boarded his wagon and they were ready to go to the Walton Ranch.

Chapter 47
Sometimes Things Go Wrong

The wagons had everything loaded up and they returned to the Walton Ranch. The vaqueros were on their horses and ready to round up the cattle. The brothers spoke to John Walton, settled up their debt and Philip shook hands with the man and thanked him for his hospitality.

Jake gave a wave to the cowboys and they unlatched the corral gates and moved the cattle out in a tight formation. The cowboys drove them to the rear of the wagons, which had already started rolling. Everything was going smoothly.

Philip and Jake were side by side and Caroline was astride them also. Soon Philip said loudly, "Hey Jake, we will be crossing Brushy Creek right north of town. I hear that cattle cross there often. It's been said that stage coaches as well as wagons often cross at that place in the creek. I also think that we will be able to see the Round Rock in the creek from which the town got the name."

Jake replied, "It sounds good, I am right with you."

In a few minutes, they saw the creek and found the spot where folks commonly crossed. That area showed lots of ruts and hoof prints. This spot seemed to be the location where most folks crossed the creek. They stopped near the creek and both men bent down to inspect the path that they would be taking. Jake said, "Well, this looks like the place."

Philip agreed and said, "Let's move the cattle across first, then the wagons." Philip and Jake drove the wagons out of the way and waved to Antonio to drive the cattle across.

The vaqueros expertly drove the herd across the creek and settled them a good distance from the creek on the other side. Philip and Jake turned the wagons toward the crossing and got the oxen moving slowly, but surely. Philip went first, and made it across safely. Next, Jake drove his wagon in the same place and everything was going well when something happened.

Jake yelled out to Philip, "Hey Philip, the left rear wheel must have found a hole in the creek bed that we didn't see." The wheel was stuck in the hole which was about one foot below the surface. The wagon couldn't move. Philip told him, "Stay where you are and we can look to figure out what the problem is and how to fix it."

Philip walked across the shallow creek and Jake climbed off his wagon and they met at the problem wheel. The water was pretty clear and they both saw the same thing at the same time. It wasn't good. The wheels on the wagons were made of wood, with wooden spokes that were attached from the rim to fasten on to the hub.

The brothers looked carefully and ran their hands down to gauge the damage to the wheel. They looked at each other with knowing glances. Philip said, "I think we know what the problem is with the wheel. The wheel must have dropped into the hole and hit a jagged rock. I'm afraid that the weight of the wagon might have been a factor. It looks like the wheel is broken pretty badly."

Philip yelled out to the cowboys, "Antonio, you and your men make a rope corral then drive the cattle into it. When the cattle are safe, come to the creek. I think we are going to need all hands on deck for this job." When the cattle were secure, the vaqueros got on their horses, rode quickly to the creek and dismounted. They walked into the creek and checked out the wheel. Antonio said, "Mr. Philip, we are going to need all of our men except one driver. It will take all of the others to lift this corner of the wagon while the oxen pull the wagon out of the creek."

Philip spoke, "Jake, you drive this thing out of here when I tell you. You will have to go slow and easy. You men help me lift this corner. When everyone is in position, I will give the order. We need to get it moved out of the creek and to flat ground, which isn't really far."

"Does everyone know what each of you is going to do?" They all nodded. Jake had taken Julia off the wagon and deposited her on dry land on the other side. Philip assisted Caroline and Albert by walking Lightning slowly and carefully across the creek.   After everyone was safely on the bank, Philip and Jake went back to the wagon. Jake got back on the wagon with the broken wheel and held the reins in his hands.

When they were in position to hold up the corner of the wagon, Philip said, "Let's go on 3, amigos." He counted "1,2,3, Go!" They worked well together as the three men lifted the corner of the wagon at the same time that Jake gently urged the oxen forward. The wagon rolled on the 3 wheels and the men had the area of the broken one. It was the left, rear wheel, Jake was right.

They got the wagon out of the creek and to flat ground. The three men had to lift and carry the wagon on the left rear of the wagon the whole way. Luckily, the banks were nearly flat. They stopped and everyone came around to look at the broken wheel. Jake said, "It's a goner, there's no way we can fix this. We are out here with no wood, and the wrong kind of tools, and we don't have a spare wheel."

Philip told the men, "We need to find a few large rocks to prop up the wagon and then take the broken wheel off. They completed those jobs. Everyone just kind of looked at the broken wheel. Their faces showed their general mood, which wasn't good.

The men got together and talked about how they could fix this mess. Jake said, "We can't fix the wheel." Antonio agreed as well as the others. Philip said, "We are going to have to find a wheelwright. I sure didn't see anything but a blacksmith shop in Round Rock. My suggestion is that two of us go to Austin with an extra horse. We will find someone who can either fix it or get a new one."

That really was the only thing they could do to get the wagon going again. Philip said, "Austin is a pretty big city now and it's only about 20 miles from here. Jake said, "Antonio and I can take 3 horses and the wheel to Austin. Philip, you need to stay with Caroline and the kids. Pedro and Jose can handle the cattle."

Philip strode over to where Caroline, Julia and Albert were sitting under a tree. Philip asked Caroline, "Do you want to go back to Round Rock to the hotel while the men are gone?" Caroline replied, "Albert and I doing very well, and the weather is good. We will stay here. You or one of the cowboys can get me back to Round Rock easily if we really need something."

Philip asked, "You honestly will tell me if you feel like you need to go to town, right?" She nodded and smiled. That lady was a pioneer woman.

Brushy Creek

Chapter 48
Just a Little Side Trip

The brothers decided that their best choice was to take the wheel to Austin. They had not seen a wheelwright on the trip since LaGrange. They determined that it should be Jake and Antonio to be the ones to go. The men removed the broken wheel. The two men saddled their horses, and took an extra horse to pack their gear and the wheel. They got on their horses and Jake said to the others, "We will be back as soon as we can." They rode off on their way to Austin.

After they left, Philip and the two cowboys, made sure that the broken wagon was secured. They moved most of the load and carried the things to a place under a live oak. They laid down a canvas tarp of the ground. Then they covered everything with another canvas tarp to protect their supplies. They pitched their tents as usual and gathered wood for the campfire. Their fortune had been serendipity. They had broken down very close to a running creek, and they could put their tents under a grove of live oak trees.

Jake and Antonio were making the best time they could without wearing out the horses. There was a trail, of sorts, to Austin. They felt like they could make it in good time. Jake said to Antonio while riding, "Rachael at the hotel said that Austin has grown to around 4000 people. We surely will be able to find someone who can fix the wheel or sell us one that will work."

Antonio spoke and said, "That sounds good, mi amigo."

It took the boys 2 days to get to Austin. There were pretty amazed at the sight they saw. Austin was located on the same

Colorado River that they had crossed near Bastrop. The city looked huge. They stopped at the first saloon they found. Ironically, it was named "The Bad Luck Saloon." They each ordered one beer and Jake asked the barkeep, "Is there a wheelwright in this city?"

The bar man, Toby, said, "You are lucky. There is a man that is a wizard with working on wheels. His name is David Kaloyan. His shed is down this same road on the right about one mile. You will see a sign hanging outside with the name 'The Broken Spoke'. He immigrated with his family when he was a boy. I think he is from Eastern Europe, Bulgaria, I believe." Jake and Antonio thanked Toby, paid up and left the saloon. They saddled up and headed down the road to find the shop.

The two went down the road and saw a building that looked like a blacksmith shop. The sign above the opening did indeed say "The Broken Spoke." Antonio told Jake, "A clever name, Si?" Jake agreed as they pulled up. They hopped down and tied their horses to a rail. There was a young man in work clothes inside the shed. He appeared to be a very young man. The guys went into the open area. The young man looked up and said, "My name is David, what can I do for you today gentlemen?" He had a strong accent, yet he spoke perfect English.

Jake told David, "We have a broken wagon wheel and are hoping that you could repair it, or sell us a new one." The three went to where the horses were tied. Jake untied the wheel from the extra horse. Antonio and Jake carried the wheel inside the shop. David said, "Put the wheel on that large table there and we'll take a look."

David looked at the wrecked wheel. David said, "You must have hit a rock with a wagon carrying a heavy load. I am sorry to say that this wheel can't be repaired. I have no wheel that will work for your wagon, but I can build you a new one in probably 4 to 5 days."

Jake replied, "We just have to have another wheel." They told David they would wait for the new wheel.

Then Jake asked, "Is there a hotel or boarding house where we can stay until the job is finished?"

David said, "Stay on this road going south and there is a clean, comfortable, boarding house on the left, in about a half mile. It is a large house that rents out rooms. You will see a sign that says, 'Rooms for Rent'."

Jake replied, "That sounds good and we will stay there and check with you each day on the progress." The guys left and checked into the boarding house.

The lady who owned the house had come down when she heard the bell ring as the door opened. Her name was Carolyn and she appeared to be a middle-aged lady. She asked the two, "Do you cowboys need to get a room?"

Jake answered, "Yes ma'am. We are having a wheel made for our wagon that has broken down. Is this your boarding house?"

Carolyn replied, "Yes, my husband and I built this house when Austin had only 400 people. He passed away and I have run this house for a long time. The city has certainly grown."

The boys' room was comfortable and clean. They checked on David's process the next day. On the second day, David told them, "I will have to cut each spoke to fit and make them sturdy. I should be finished with the spokes in a couple of days. I will have to set the spokes with glue and nails. They will have to dry over night, so it should be ready in four days."

Jake said with a friendly voice, "That will be fine and thank you."The guys left and went to a small café to eat and have a beer. They returned to the boarding house and settled in their rented beds. The guys slept well that night.

The next morning, they had breakfast at the café and headed out to check on the progress of the wheel. They stopped and went into the shop. David said, "Good timing, I have finished making the last spoke. Then I can set it in the rim of the wheel. I have set all the other spokes in to the hub and rim already. It takes a little time but I want to make sure it will be a sturdy wheel.

Antonio said "gracias," and they headed back to the house.

The men woke up the next morning, ate a good breakfast, and then rode to 'The Broken Spoke'. When they got to the shop, David told them, "I have made each piece and have inserted each spoke. It is finished, but I think we need to give it one more night to make sure the glue has set and dried. It should be ready to roll tomorrow."

The next morning, the guys checked out of the boarding house and thanked Carolyn for her hospitality. They then packed their gear and rode to The Broken Spoke. David told them, "Well there is your new wheel. It should give you service for a long time." They settled the payment with David. They then tied the new wheel to the spare horse, and said their farewells. They mounted their horses and started back to the temporary camp where the other folks were.

They camped for two nights on the way back. The guys finally got to the Smith camp on the third day. They were tired, but relieved that they had finished their journey. As they got close enough to see the camp, they waved and whistled. Everyone at the camp waved back. They reached the camp and were glad to get off their horses. There were happy greetings all around. Philip said "Good job men. Now we can get back to the trip tomorrow."

Chapter 49
On Our Way Home

They had attached the new wheel on the afternoon that the guys returned. Everything worked perfectly with the wheel and they loaded the wagons to leave in the morning. They had their customary talk around the campfire, and Jake and Antonio told them of their trip. Everyone got up with the Sun and they were ready to go. The vaqueros had the cattle rounded up and they were also ready. The caravan left and headed to the Chisholm Trail. The weary travelers were on the final leg of their amazing adventure. They made good time and covered a few miles on the first day.

It would take 3 to 4 more days to reach their goal. They had entered the edge of what is called "The Hill Country." It was beautiful terrain, and there were more hills than they had traversed so far. On the second day, Philip noticed seven or eight Indian braves riding parallel with the wagons. They were barely in sight, and most of the time he couldn't see them at all.

At the campfire that night, Philip spoke with a little tension in his voice. He asked, "Did anyone else see the Indians shadowing us today?" No one answered as they looked around. Philip said, "They didn't look like they were going to come after us, but they certainly knew where we were. We need to have watch tonight. I think they are Comanches. By my reckoning, we should be at our new home by tomorrow. Get a good night's sleep." They all went to sleep early except the man on watch, and everyone was excited that they were finally going to be home.

It was mid afternoon when everyone came to a stop. Philip pointed and said, "This is going to be our home." He pointed toward a tree line that was following the Lampasas River. Everyone hooted and smiled, except for Albert, of course. They had made it to "The Promised Land." It was a serene and beautiful location. The natural grass was about 4 feet tall and waving in the wind. The travelers drove down toward the river, and set up camp on their own land for the very first time. They had arrived at their destination on September 16th, 1854.

Chapter 50
Settlers at Last

The first thing they did when they reached the ranch was to set up camp as they had done for the previous four months. They pitched the tents, untied the oxen, and built a temporary corral for the cattle. Jake said, "Well, this is just the same as we have done before."

Caroline replied, "Dear Jake, the only important difference is that this is our own land, now and forever."

That made Jake smile. He had a funny look on his face when he started fumbling around inside his pack. He finally brought his hand out of the pack and he was hiding something behind his back. He reached out his hand and offered the piece of paper to Caroline.

Caroline carefully took the paper from Jake and held it in front of her face. She gazed at the illustration in her sight. Her face turned from a bewildered one to a face full of joy. She was looking at the sketch that Jake had drawn of her and the new born baby, Albert, cuddled against her chest. Jake had drawn this picture at the campfire on the night that Albert was born.

He had not shown it to anyone until this moment. Caroline began crying tears of joy. Through the tears, she said to Jake, "This is one of the most amazing sights I have ever seen. In a quiet, sincere voice she added, "Thank you dear Jake. I will treasure this drawing as long as I live."

The travelers had a good night's sleep and woke up energized. They sat around the morning campfire and were just rambling on and on. Jake said "The first thing I am going to do is find wood and build a real shelter. I am then going to build a bed to sleep in."

Philip said, "It is so fulfilling to reach such a grand goal as we have achieved. I too will build a shelter, and get to work on a real house."

The next day, Philip and Jake went to their hidden bank on the under board of one of the wagons. They counted out the amount they had promised the cattle drovers. Jake said to Philip, "Hey brother, these guys were more than workers, they were family. They actually saved our lives down by LaGrange. I suggest that we give them all a bonus, since they are good men with families."

Philip agreed, "I think that gesture is certainly the right thing to do."

They called Antonio, Jose, and Pedro over to the wagon. Philip said to them, "We couldn't have done this without you vaqueros. Here are your wages, and we hope to see you again."

Antonio spoke and said, "Senor Smith, it was our honor to work together with you and your wonderful family. We have discussed it, and we are going to stay until we can help you build a sturdy corral for your cattle. We do not want any extra pay for that because we feel like until we get those cattle safely corralled, we haven't finished our job."

Philip and Jake both thanked them, and hugged each one. Philip spoke, "You guys don't really know how important you were to us on the trip. Also how much we care about you. We hope to come to Monterey and meet your families some day. I have also written this paper for each you to present to your next boss. It is called a reference. It simply states the truth about you guys. It says that you are honest, hard working men, who finish a job and will do whatever is needed. I have signed it, and stated the address where they can mail any request to me if they wish."

That day, the guys worked together to build a suitable shelter for Jake. They chopped down the appropriate sized trees to build a rudimentary log cabin. Jake's place was near the river. It took them four days to obtain the logs and drag them to Jake's spot. It took them three more days to put the shelter together. It had to be water proof, and they put the logs together with mud as the Indians did with adobe.

Jake built his bed and used his blankets that he had brought for his mattress. He had a simple door and an outside fire pit. The roof was constructed of wood and adobe mixed with leaves. It was a livable place until he could build a stronger house on his land. In the meantime the others slept in Jake's shelter.

After building Jake's cabin, they started up on the house for Philip, Caroline, Julia and Albert. This structure would be located about a half of a mile from the river. The cowboys were doing their own work building a sturdy corral for the cattle. Philip had ridden to the corral and said, "It seems like it's almost finished. You guys seem to always amaze me, no matter what you are working on."

The folks began working on Philip's house. It was going to be built mostly of adobe. This house would survive on the same spot for a very long time. The vaqueros came to the building site to say goodbye. Antonio spoke first saying, "We have been honored to be with your family for this long journey and we will never forget you."

Philip asked, "What will you do next?"

Antonio said, "We will return to our homes, and stay for a visit with our families for awhile. Then we will ride back to Matagorda and find work herding cattle." Philip retrieved the bag and replied, "We will hold the gold coins until you leave."

Jake spoke this time and said, "We agreed that you three have more than earned your money. We will then pay you when you finish the corral. And we want to thank you guys in helping us along the journey." Before they left, Antonio had approach Philip. He told Philip that "Pedro has a very important question to ask you and Jake." Philip was wondering what Pedro wanted to ask about. Antonio waved for Pedro to come. He did, and Antonio told Philip and Jake that "I would like to interpret what Pedro has to ask."

Jake answered, "Of course that will be okay."

In Spanish mostly, Pedro got the courage to ask the brothers his question. Antonio interpreted Pedro's words.

Antonio asked the question of Pedro, in English. He told the brothers that "Pedro would like to know if he could move back here, and be a ranch hand or ranch manager. He loves this place, and you people. Would you consider having he and his wife come back to live on the ranch?"

Pedro spoke to the brothers with Antonio translating his words. "My wife and I only have one child, a son. The son is already grown and has a good job and has his own family. We would be happy here with me and my wife, Felicia. We will build our own house and take care of the land, landscape, and animals. Felicia can help with the children, and she is a very good cook." Antonio translated the words perfectly in English.

Philip and Jake walked out of hearing distance. Philip said, "We could use extra help and he's a good worker and a good man.

Jake said, "I agree, but what if we don't start earning money with the farm and the beef?"

Philip replied to Jake, "It will all work out." Philip this time looked at Pedro and asked Antonio to translate. Philip, speaking in English said, "Well, Pedro, we couldn't get more of a perfect piece of the puzzle. We surely will love to have .you and your wife come back, and live here. When you return, you will be our ranch manager."

Caroline spoke and said "It will be a pleasure having someone else to help. Soon, Julia will be cooking, and our family is growing. I would really like to have some help."

Jake said to Pedro, with Antonio translating, "We will pay for your services, and a place for you and your wife to stay." Antonio, who was still translating for Jake said, "Now saddle up and we will give you your wages earned. Pedro, go get your wife. If she is for this, you two are welcome to come and live on The Smith Ranch. But I advise you to work a little bit on your English during your trip. Antonio won't be here when you get back." Both men laughed, although Pedro knew it was true.

Jake called all the vaqueros together. He told them "Philip and I agreed to give you a bonus for the excellent work you've done."

Philip spoke up and added, "You men are very honorable and you literally saved the lives of us and our family. We wish you every good thing in your lives, and thank you with all our hearts."

Two amigos said, "Gracias" as they sped off on their horses riding south. Philip had asked Pedro to wait behind.

When the others rode off, Philip said to Pedro, "We have made a deal Pedro, but life can give us many changes. I wish you the very best, but would certainly understand if you stay with your family in Mexico. Either way is fine for us. I hope to see you two riding up to the ranch someday soon."

The men shook hands, and looked at each other in the eyes. Pedro took his money, hopped on his horse, and then without saying a word or looking back, he started off to catch up with his friends. One of the Mexican ranch hands translated

Philip's remarks. The vaqueros were bound for Monterey. Philip realized that he had become brothers with the three amigos.

Julia had watched what happened and asked her father, "Will those nice men ever come back to see us?" Philip had a forlorn look on his face when he answered quietly, "I sure do hope so, I surely do. Mr. Pedro is probably going to go to his home, get his wife, and then come back to live here.

Julia was very happy with that news. She had seen a lot on the journey, and had formed a relationship with the vaqueros. She liked Pedro the most. Mostly because, even though she couldn't understand him, he played with her, did card tricks, and played music to entertain her. She was so glad that she might see him again.

The settlers were self sufficient and able to have fresh clean water, plenty of game, and they planted wheat and oats for themselves and their animals. They had to build a primitive plow for the oxen to pull behind in order to sow their seeds.

The pasture they were living in provided plenty of feed for the cattle, as well as having enough abundance to have hay bales. Each day, they would drive the cattle down to the river for water and carry back some to fill a wooden trough they had made. They soon built a viaduct with a way to pump water from the river up to a trough that could hold water for all the animals. They *were* settlers and *cattle ranchers*.

The nearest town to the ranch was known as Burleson. It is about 15 miles south of the ranch. The town was named for John Burleson, who was awarded 1280 acres for his service in the Revolutionary War. He decided to claim his land in what is now named Lampasas. The area had seven mineral springs and the name gradually become Lampasas Springs. The town of Lampasas was officially named Lampasas, when the

County of Lampasas was created in 1856. The city was incorporated as Lampasas in 1883.(6)

There are a few theories regarding the origin of the name, Lampasas. The majority believes that the name was based on the Spanish Aquyo Expedition in 1721. Spanish explorers discovered the river and called it the Lampazos River.(6) Many think that Lampasas is an English version of a town in Mexico named Lampazos, which is a beautiful city with many springs.

Chapter 51
Good News from Home

On a cool clear night, in November, 1854, the settlers were around the campfire. They kept their tradition and gathered each night unless it was raining or very cold. Jake said, "This sky is amazing. There must be 10,000 stars in the sky. And look at that moon, beautiful."

Caroline said, "That is a remarkable sky. I am so pleased that we had our journey, and we have a wonderful place to work and live for the rest of our lives." Philip seemed to have had a smile on his face all day. He hadn't said much, and now he was to the point of spilling out his great news. He spoke, "Well folks, I have some news. As you know, I have been gone for two days as I went to visit the town of Burleson for some supplies."

After I got what we needed, I decided to check the post office. I just had a hunch. Low and behold, the postmaster handed me a letter addressed to me, through General Delivery. I tore it open and wondered who had sent it. I will read it to you all,"

"Dear family, Hello to Philip, Caroline, Jacob, Jr., Julia, and, there should be a little one where you are. Elizabeth and I are well as are your siblings. After much conversation, we have decided to sell our section up there. We love our ranch and also decided that you poor folks must not have very much money. I know there are many things that could help you that you can't yet afford yet."

"We realized that we want to stay in our home here in Matagorda. We hope to come see you, but, we are getting older, and it might not be possible. We would love it if you could come down

sometime, but we also know how difficult that would be. We know you are well and happy. I have enclosed a check from the bank in the amount most of the sale price. We thought you could use some new things. We pray for you every day and miss you more than you can know. Oma and Opa send all our love." The letter was signed Jacob Smith, Sr. and Elizabeth Smith. There was a P.S. from Elizabeth, *"A special kiss from grandma Liz to you all, and please tell Julia to kiss and squeeze that sweet little Dolly for me.'"*

A silence came over the family. Here they were, under the open sky, yet feeling like they were right there with their loved ones. Everyone was crying silently, even the tough guy Jake. At that moment, both Caroline and Julia began to cry aloud, as tears poured from their eyes like a thunder cloud with all the rain pouring down at one time.

As the crying subdued, there became the loudest silence that could ever be. Philip watched and was silent himself for what seemed to be an eternity. He finally spoke up, "I have never had a check in my life. I didn't even know what it was. I took it to the bank. That was only the second time I had ever been in a bank, the other time was with papa.

I showed the check to the bank teller, Christa Anderson. I asked her "What exactly is this, and how do I use it?" Miss Anderson said, "You have a few options. You can cash the whole amount and receive the entire amount in currency or gold coins. Or, you could put some of the amount in a savings account, so you will have a nest egg in a safe place for the future."

Jake asked, "O.K. boss, what did you do?"

Philip said, "I put $100 in a savings account, so that any of us can withdraw from the account at anytime. The rest I got in gold coins." His brother and wife were flabbergasted. They just grinned from ear to ear.

Philip said, "I've got something to show you folks." He then went to the wagon and pulled out a bag. With glee in his eyes, he poured out all the coins at their feet. They all started dancing around the fire and whooping it up at the same time. Philip spoke again, "Now come with me." They followed him to the wagon which was covered with a tarp. With their eyes as opened as they could be, they wondered what would come next.

Philip went to the tarp with his arms spread, grabbed the tarp by the corners and threw it off the load. There were gasps when the item was revealed. There, lying in the back of the wagon, was a brand new, store bought, modern plow. It had a tiller forged from steel, and the hitch was also reinforced with steel. Nobody could speak. Yes, it was Jake who spoke first and said with a bit of laughter in his voice, "Well, that thing should last us until we still want to use it, but have become too feeble to move it." What a joyful night.

Horse drawn plow, circa1850s

Chapter 52
Getting Settled

The Smiths were hard workers. They worked from dawn to dusk as they had their whole life. The vaqueros had worked extra every day to build a strong, sturdy corral for the horses, cattle and oxen. Philip and Jake were working on building the two houses for the brothers.

Philip spoke up, mostly talking to Caroline, "While I was in town, I not only came home with the plow, but I have brought winter vegetable seeds so that we have more than meat, milk and pecans from our native grove. I talked to folks to see what would grow in the winter here. I have seeds for turnips, collard greens, cabbage, and rutabaga. Caroline said, "I can plow the rows for the vegetables while Julia can watch Albert. I will have them in sight at all times, and I know how to sow seeds. Also, the rows will not need to be very deep since the horse or ox does all the work."

Philip didn't put up any fight. He had personally watched his wife plow many acres back home. He said, "I'm O.K. with it and it seems like the baby will be well supervised. I would like to build the main house to be one that will survive longer than we do."

Philip continued, "There is a mill near Goldthwaite, which is about 25 miles from here on the road from Burleson, which is a good road. I plan to buy beams and sheets of wood for the house. The exterior of our updated house will have walls of limestone that is 2 feet wide. I have put in an order while I was in town. There will include a couple of custom stones and they will be delivered in a short time. These stones will give the house strength and insulation in the walls. We can build a bedroom for Jake if he is willing, and no one objects."

Caroline said with a wry look, "I don't know if I can deal with your brother," and turned and gave a wink to Jake. He winked back.

Chapter 53
Get Some Materials We Will Need

That night, Philip told Caroline before going to bed, "Hey angel, how would you and little Albert like to go to Mills County with me to get some supplies?"

Caroline opened her very large eyes and said, "That is where my brother John, and your sister Emily live. They moved to Mills County after they got married."

Philip said, "That's what I was thinking. I know we both would enjoy seeing our siblings for the first time since our weddings."

Caroline's eyes began to water and she threw herself against Philip and just started kissing him. He finally needed to get some air, so he gently pushed her back and said, "Well I guess that was a 'Yes'."

"Julia is a big girl now and Jake is the best babysitter around," Caroline stated. "Little Albert is still very small and I am still breast feeding. We will be fine too." They both seemed very calm and happy.

Philip said, "We will go tomorrow and hope to find the Russlers." They ended the conversation with a sweet kiss. They snuggled all night, that night.

The next morning, Philip, Caroline, and Albert got the wagon ready to go to Mills County. They packed up the things that they might need for the trip. They inspected everything and climbed on the driver's bench. Jake, holding Albert, had come out to the wagon to wish them well. He handed the child to Caroline and said, "Well folks, I know you are going to have a smooth, easy trip. Be careful though, there are Indians and bandits out there."

Philip replied with a bit of sarcasm with the words, "You just take care of the kid and yourself."

Jake replied, "You do realize that I single handedly fought off 14 bandits that were attacking us. This should be easy enough."

Philip broke out with a belly laugh, and said, "Oh, you are such a dangerous gunslinger."

They all laughed and Philip and Caroline waved and said, "See you soon." And off they went.

They were traveling on the ox wagon north to Mills County. It would be a fairly quick trip since they had no load. Philip had tied Lightning and another horse to the back of the wagon. Coming back with a full load would be quite different. They enjoyed being together with no one else around. It was actually a nice trip and they enjoyed the scenery. The road was well worn and the wagon provided a rather smooth ride.

They reached the mill, which was a couple of miles south of Goldthwaite. It only took them two nights to reach the mill. They stopped at the mill and went in. Philip was amazed to see saws and equipment that he had never seen before. They were met with a strong, young man named Tyler. He spoke while holding his hand out to shake Philip's hand saying, "Howdy, how can I help you today?"

Philip shook his hand and stated, "I am Philip Smith, a settler, and my family moved from Germany to Texas in 1833. This is my wife, Caroline and our baby, Albert. We have just settled land down the road from here, near Burleson."

Tyler spoke and asked Philip, "What will you be looking for?"

Philip replied, "We will need 15 beams cut about 18-20 feet long. They will all need to be the same length however. We also need two more hammers, and probably two boxes of those wooden pegs and nails. We truly are in wild country. I could use a better saw for the cedar and oaks."

Tyler told him, "You're in luck, we have beams that came from the Colorado River, and they have already been cut. If you're going to cut trees at all, I surely advise you get a two handle saw. Come with me and take a look."

They walked to the saws. Philip said, "I've never seen anything like that."

Tyler then told them, "We get these from Minnesota from a man named Jim Normann. We are friends, and he sells them at a very good price. As long as you have someone willing to work with you, you won't believe how fast you can cut trees or beams. Ty then took him to the lumber yard and showed Philip their stock of beams. Philip was impressed and he said, "Those beams will work very well for us."

Tyler had a writing pad and wrote everything down. Philip picked up a few more things that he might need. Ty told Philip the cost of the final bill. Philip was satisfied. Tyler told him, "I will have my men carry the beams to your wagon. Would you mind driving the wagon around to the back? Please park it as close to the beams as you can get it." The men shook hands over the deal and Philip went to the wagon to drive it around to the back yard. He met with Tyler in the lumber yard.

Philip told Tyler, "On another issue, we are looking to visit our siblings, John and Emily Russler. Emily is my sister, and John is my wife's brother. When they left Matagorda they headed for Scallorn, here in Mills County. They were planning to be cattle ranchers like us. Do you know them, and where they might live?"

Tyler said, "Yes Sir, John was in this very shop yesterday buying some tools. You would be welcome to leave your wagon and oxen here while you visit your kin. You could park them under the shed, and we could feed and water the oxen if needed."

Philip replied, "That's fine, we have our two horses. We will go to visit our relatives and the horses will make it much easier. Thank you Tyler."

Ty told them, "They live down this road. Turn right leaving the mill and it is the road to Scallorn. Their ranch is a mile or two short of the town. They have a large Texas Flag outside, you can't miss it. And while you're going that way, could you please take this box of nails that he needed, and we just got them in today."

Philip replied, "I'd be happy to take them to John."

Caroline replied, "It was a pleasure to meet you, and thank you for taking care of our needs."

Ty quietly tipped his hat and said, "Good to meet you two, and I'll have everything you need in a couple of days." Philip and Caroline mounted their horses. Ty lifted Albert into the cradleboard and tightened it just enough. It seemed as if he had done this before. Ty said, "Adios for now, and we'll see you in a couple of days. Be careful and stay safe."

They turned to the right when they left the mill and rode off down the main road. Caroline had brought some snacks and they both believed that they would not have to camp tonight. The two were certainly more comfortable on horseback instead of sitting and getting bumped around on the wagon. They had been home sick, but knowing that they would see their siblings would be a joy for all. The Smiths had no way of telling the Russlers that they were coming. They would have to surprise them when they reached their ranch.

Philip, Caroline and Albert headed down the road with Philip riding his old friend, Lightning. Albert was comfortably snug in his cradleboard. They had one quick break while

Caroline fed the baby, and the horses got some water. Philip had brought some carrots for the animals. After a few minutes they mounted their steeds and continued their ride. They saw a group of Indians that were going parallel to them. Philip told her, "I saw a group of them a few days before we arrived at School Creek. I'm pretty sure it is a Comanche raiding party.

A man in town told me that the tribe was run out of the territory by U.S. Horse Soldiers. He said that most of them went up north, and were forced to live on a reservation. Several of the braves and their women escaped and were not captured. Bands like these still roam this country. The guy said that mostly they are trying to steal horses, and usually don't want a conflict. He did state in a very serious tone however, "Be on the alert when they are around. It's said that there can be very deadly."

Philip instinctively gripped his holstered gun and asked Caroline, "Do you have your rifle and hand gun loaded, just in case?"

She responded, "I sure do." They continued on the short trip to be with their family that they hadn't seen for a couple of years.

Philip shouted out, "There is the Texas flag ahead, we have made it." They rode a few more yards and turned into the dirt road where the flag was flying. Philip and Caroline rode up to the house. They dismounted, got Albert, and walked quickly to the door and knocked. The door opened and Emily looked shocked. She could barely get a word out of her mouth. Then she yelled, "Philip! Is that really you?" She turned her head around and yelled toward the back of the house, "John, we've got company!"

John hollered back, "Be right there Hon." By the time he got to the front door, Emily was hugging all three of her kin. She said, "I thought we might never see you folks again, and a baby to boot." The smile on her face seemed to be stuck forever. Caroline replied, "You know our Julia, our precious daughter. She stayed at the ranch with Jake. This little one is Albert, the traveler. Philip's brother Jake came with us on our journey from Matagorda. We settled near the Lampasas River and have settled in quite well. Jake is taking care of everything."

Right about then, John was at the front door and hooted out, "Holy smoke, my sister and her family! Thank you Lord!" Pretty soon John was hugging everyone and had a smile as great as Emily's. Emily said, "Come into our modest home right now, and let's get caught up." They all went into the living area and had a seat. Caroline had unpacked Albert and let him crawl on the rug.

Emily asked, "John, fetch Little John from the back, and bring him in here to meet his aunt, uncle, and cousin."

John continued toward the back door saying, "Little John was named John Russler, Jr., and he just turned 5 years old."

Emily spoke up and said, "We nick-named him, 'Little John', so the right John would respond to me. We also got a little kick about him having the moniker of 'Little John' of the legend of Robin Hood."

In just a couple of minutes, John and Little John appeared at the back door. As they came into the living area, Emily told Little John, "Lil John, I want you to meet your Uncle Philip, Aunt Caroline, and your cousin, Albert." Lil John ran to these people he had never met and hugged each one with all his might. He said, "Are you going to live with us?" He asked.

Philip responded, "I'm don't think we can young nephew. We will stay for a few nights, but we also came to buy supplies from the mill. After that we will have to go home.

But, we sure are glad to meet you. You look just like your dad. Maybe your family can come visit our place."

Philip remembered the nails and handed them to John, and said, "Tyler asked me to bring these to you."

John grinned and said a heart-felt 'thank you'.

Emily explained to the boy, "Philip is my brother and Caroline is your dad's sister. Albert is your first cousin. In this case, you are a double nephew. You don't see that very much. We all used to live on your grandpa's ranch down by the ocean." Little John had a most concerned look on his face. He said, "I am so pleased to meet my relatives. The other kids all talk about their relatives, and now I can talk about mine." At barely 5 years old, the parents were not really sure how much he had understood. It was obvious that the child was very happy to meet the Smiths.

The Smiths stayed for 3 nights with their kin. Philip and John went to the mill the next day on horseback and Caroline and Albert stayed with Little John and Emily.

When Philip and John arrived at the mill, they went inside and greeted Tyler. Philip had picked out the beams and boards that he needed to finish building their house. They left the wagon at the mill and returned to the Russler home. Philip, Caroline and Albert would ride to the mill the next day on horseback. Tyler had told Philip that he would have the wagon loaded and ready to go.

They got home to the Russler house in a short time. The visitors and hosts had a grand time being with each other and getting even closer to one another. On the third day, Philip said, "We sure appreciate the hospitality, and being with you folks. We sure do hope that you can return the visit and please stay with us sometime." Philip drew John a basic map of how to get to their place, and handed it to John. His sister's husband smiled and hugged his brother-in-law.

The next morning, the Smiths said goodbye to John, Emily and Little John. The families waved and the visitors left for the mill to fetch the wagon. They arrived at the mill after a short ride. Philip found Tyler, and the owner asked them to come inside and have some refreshment. They ate some baked bread and pie, and enjoyed some really good coffee. Ty walked them out front and they saw that the wagon was already hitched up and ready to leave. Philip tied the horses to the back of the wagon. He settled up the cost with Ty. The Smiths gave their thanks to Tyler, and boarded the wagon. The family was heading back to the ranch. Philip said to Caroline, "Well, we've bought us a bunch of work back there." Caroline just looked him somewhat perplexed, and showed a very big smile.

They had to camp one night before they got home, due to the heavy load in the wagon. At the campfire, Philip seemed to be at peace. He looked at Caroline and said, "You know, it isn't often that we three are alone together." Albert was on Caroline's lap, and she said, "This is what I hoped for when we decided to settle our land. It is the serenity and being together."

Philip said, "We need to take Julia and Albert and have a family camp out soon." Caroline, as usual, smiled and gazed into Philip's eyes with her piercing blue eyes. All was well.

Chapter 54
The Chisholm Trail

The three Smiths were very pleased when they saw their ranch the next day. Jake was standing out by the barn waving heartily when he saw the wagon coming down the road. Philip waved back, and they parked the wagon. Jake greeted them as they got off the wagon and asked, "Hey Philip, do you want me to help you unload the wagon?" Philip replied, "No thanks Jake, it is a cloudless evening and it most likely will not rain tonight. We are tired, and we can gather up some help from the ranch hands to unload the beams tomorrow."

The next day, the beams were moved next to where the present house was standing. Philip said, "Well, this is a major step toward making this a house that will outlive us. Our next step will be to obtain large limestone blocks for the walls. That will be an effort that will be significant."

Jake had to say something, and replied, "Oh Philip, you and I can build this house in a few days," chuckling the whole time.

Between the Smith boys, the vaqueros, friends, neighbors, and ranch hands, the men had built large cattle corrals. Philip knew most of the cattlemen that passed through here. It included Means and Evans, Cooksie, Townsens, Senterfitt, and others who would drive their cattle on this trail. All the cattlemen knew Philip well. The cowboys knew that if they could make it to Philip's corrals by nightfall, they would be welcome to hold their cattle for the overnight. They also knew that they would have a good meal and a comfortable place to sleep. Some would even stay for a few days.(1)

The ranch was located on a trail that was a feeder of the Chisholm Trail. This part of the trail was used by cattle drives from the south, and the trail would merge into the major Chisholm Trail farther north. The drives were destined to end in Kansas, where the cattle bosses would sell the cattle. Kansas City had elaborate train terminals where the Texas cattle could be transported to many destinations across the country.

Philip himself would sometimes have cattle drives when his herds had gotten too large. He normally would drive a few head to auction. They would drive the cows to the nearest town that was holding an auction. Sometimes the boss of a cattle drive would buy a few head of cattle from Philip and Jake when they stopped. There were a couple of bulls and a few heifers that Philip would not sell. He would keep these cattle for breeding purposes.

It was getting into autumn and things had settled down. Philip was making great strides on building his house. It would be the home he had always wanted to have. Caroline had begun to till the rows for her vegetables and Philip, Jake, and the hands had really started making it a fine ranch. The cattle were reproducing and everything was well.

A few cattle drives had come by to stay for a day or two, and Philip loved the company. He also would question the trail boss for tips on cattle ranching, although he probably knew as much as any of them. He had a lot of experience while he was living and working on his father's ranch. Philip always did have a desire to learn, ever since he was a small boy. One night at dinner, the family spoke of the many good people that had stopped at the ranch.

Chapter 55
The Unimaginable

Beside the cattle drives stopping off at Philip's place, sometimes families would stop while traveling to their destination. One bright, sunny day, early in October, 1854, a family appeared in a covered wagon that was approaching the house. It was the Walker family. The father, Bob Walker, saw the place and drove up to Philip's house. He and his family were exhausted. He parked the wagon, and he, his wife and his 15 year old son and their 5 year old daughter got off the wagon.

Philip came out of the house as the Walkers walked toward the front door. They met up, and Philip said, "Welcome strangers, Philip Smith here, welcome to our ranch." Bob and Philip both reached their hands out to shake. Bob replied, "I'm Bob Walker, this is my wife, Lottie, my son, Billy, and my daughter, Abigail. We are immigrants from England and we arrived in Matagorda.

We stayed for awhile, then we moved to Victoria to take a job. My family came to Texas about 6 years ago. Abigail is our first child to be born in the U.S., and the only American citizen by birth in our family. I have been working in Victoria since we got there. Work is hard to find, and the pay is not great."

Philip told him, "My family also landed in Matagorda, and my father has owned a cattle ranch in the peninsula since 1833. I was 12 years old at that time, and I stayed on the ranch until 1854. I married Caroline and we stayed on the ranch for a couple of years. We decided to leave the coast and become settlers in central Texas. It was a tough journey getting here to settle. Bob, what drove you to come to Texas?"

Bob said, "I came from a poor family of farm workers in southwest England."

"We have read and heard about the gold rush in northern California," Bob told him. "We gathered everything we needed, and sold the rest. We have decided to go to California and either pan, or mine for gold. The big rush started in 1849, but people are, to this day, still striking it rich."

Philip said to them, "We have shelter where you can sleep, and food for you to eat. You're welcome to stay for a while if you want. He went to the door and called Caroline, Jake, and Julia to come out front. When they appeared, Philip told the Walkers, "This is my sweet wife, Caroline, my brother, and best friend, Jake, our daughter, Julia, and our little one, Albert."

The Walker family introduced themselves, and then they were accompanied by Philip and Jake. The brothers showed the Walkers where they could sleep that night. Philip told them, "Unload whatever you need. There are blankets and pillows, and this room can sleep all of you. There is a shared bath in that larger house. You can heat water on a wood stove there."

Philip continued, "Often there are cattle men sleeping in this cabin. You came at the right time, because there are no cattle drives lately. You have the run of the place. Our ranch hands have their own structures that they live in. Please come over to the house around 6 o'clock and eat supper with us."

It was getting late in the afternoon and the Walkers showed up at the house right before six. The Smiths let them in and the house smelled wonderful. Caroline and Julia had been cooking chicken and dumplings for about an hour. Philip had bought a few chickens a while back, and the guys built an adequate chicken pen out by the barn. They had allowed several hens to lay fertilized eggs, and this allowed them to double their stock of chickens. They enjoyed a surplus of chickens to eat as well as the eggs.

Philip called out, "Time to eat folks." Everyone gathered around the large dinner table and Philip said a prayer. Everyone sat down as Caroline, Julia, and Lottie served the meal. There were happy conversations, and then Billy spoke up saying, "Dad, can I borrow your rifle tomorrow and try to kill a deer for dinner?"

Bob said, "Sure Bill, you are competent with a gun." Bob could tell that Billy would like to do something to feel like an adult. Philip spoke to Billy saying, "Hey young Bill, I will loan you a horse to go along with the one you will be riding. And, plenty of rope to tie the deer to the spare horse to bring the deer back. I also will loan you a saddle that has a rifle holster attached." Billy's eyes were twinkling with joy as he was trying to subdue the biggest smile he had ever remembered.

The Smiths enjoyed the company of their new friends and, when it got dark, the Walkers retired to their lodging. Philip said, "Please join us for breakfast tomorrow morning when you get up."

Bob replied, "Thank you for your hospitality, and we surely needed the rest. We will see you in the morning."

After breakfast, the men went to the barn with Billy. His dad gave him the gun and Philip had a horse saddled. Billy took the gun from his dad and he put the gun in the holster. Philip also had another horse with a halter on, and extra rope. Philip handed the boy his sharp knife which was also in a holster. Philip told Billy, "Put it on your belt. I keep this with me outside wherever I go. I'll loan it to you until you get back. It might come in handy."

His father said, "Be careful, watch your surroundings and good luck son."

Philip told Billy with a very stern look, "Billy, there are Comanche Indians that are nomadic in this area. Their goal is to steal horses, and it provides a brave with wealth in their culture. We have never seen any Comanches on our land, but we have seen them in the general area. Billy just grinned as he mounted the horse and Philip handed the rope tied to the halter.

"Good hunting Billy, and keep your eyes open, there could be trouble out there, and if you even get a glimpse of any Indians, get back to the ranch as fast as you can and shoot a rifle into the air to alert us." The boy mounted his horse and took off toward the river, with the extra horse in tow.

The Lampasas River was less than a mile from the barn, and it had tree lines on both sides of the river. Bob told Philip, "I would love to help you with any work you need to do."

Philip replied, "I've been working to make my original shelter into a real house, and would love some help."

The men had been working for an hour and they both heard a rifle report from down by the river. Philip said, "He must have seen a deer and took a shot." Bob replied, "Well, we only heard one shot, so he either missed and the deer ran, or it was a clean shot. It also could have been a warning shot. We will find out soon enough." The men continued their work on the house.

The men had worked for about another hour when Bob said, "It's been a long time since we heard the shot, do you think something could be wrong?"

Philip said, "Although it hasn't been long, I too think we should go check on the boy." Philip was also concerned about Billy. They decided that the men should go find Billy.

Philip said to Bob, "Well, let's go down to the river and see if he's all right." Philip whistled at Jake and waved him over. Jake scurried over to the barn where the other two men were. Philip told him, "Bob's son, Billy, left to hunt after breakfast. We heard a rifle shot and figured he missed a deer. We have been waiting for him to come back, but he hasn't returned. We plan to go down and check things out. Would you like to come with us?"

Jake said, "Of course, you guys saddle up and I will get an extra horse just in case we need one."

The men mounted their horses and took off toward the river. It took only a short time to reach it. As they got close to the river, there was a lot of brush, and they tied their horses to some small trees when they reached the brush. Jake was a good scout, and could spot signs well. He said, "Well, it looks like Billy walked two horses down to the water. You see how there are small broken branches, and I see a few of the horses prints. The guys worked their way through the brush, and Bob was yelling out Billy's name as they descended toward the river.

When they got through the brush, there was a bank that was 4 to 5 feet down to the river. There were some paths to get down, so they went down to the water. The river had deep pools, as well as shallow rocky spots. At the edge of the river, there was walking room on both sides due to the river being at a slow, fairly shallow state. There had not been any heavy rains lately.

Jake said, I'll go upstream and you guys go downstream. Holler if you see anything. If we get beyond hearing distance and you see evidence of Billy, shoot one shot into the air. I will do the same. If we don't hear a shot, meet back here in 15 minutes."

They split up and went their different ways. After about 5 minutes, Jake saw the prints of two horses and he decided it was Billy's horses. He shot his pistol one time, and continued following the trail. He was getting worried because he came to spot where there were several horse tracks, most without shoes, and the two that Billy had which were shod.

While he waited for the other two, he looked around with a keen eye. He saw something just inside the brush line and went to see what it was. When he got close enough, he let out a loud gasp. It was Billy's body, with five arrows in him. He went to the body to check to see if he was still alive. There was no breath or heart beat.

Jake turned white, and his brain was struggling at what his eyes and mind were trying to understand. He figured out quickly that Billy had been ambushed by Indians. He was dizzy, but he realized what had happened. He had to let his father know what had happened. He pulled the arrows out of Billy, and broke each one, then threw them as far as he could into the brush. He walked back toward the others trying to calm down and think of what he was going to say. About that time, he saw Philip and Bob from a distance and they were closing in quickly toward him.

They met on the riverbank, and Philip asked him, "Did you find something?" Philip could tell something was wrong, because he had seen that look on Jake's face before. Jake said, "You guys sit down for a minute on that big rock."

They did, and Bob asked Jake with a loud nervous voice, "Jake, is my boy all right? Have you seen him?" Jake steadied himself inside and out. He sat down next to Bob and slowly, and quietly spoke to the father, "Bob, it is bad news, Billy is gone, he was killed."

Bob yelled back at Jake, "What do you mean? He's gone! He can't be."

Jake sat next to Bob and put his arm around Bob's shoulder and said, "Bob, I am so sorry to tell you that he was killed." Bob was in shock and very confused and his face had turned ashen. Bob asked Jake in a quieter, calmer way, "Are you telling me that my boy is dead?" Jake nodded. Bob started shaking and sobbing and couldn't get any words out. When he had calmed down some, he asked Jake, "Where is he, and what happened to him?"

Jake stood and said, "Let me show you where he is." They walked upstream for several feet, and then the men could see the boy's body. Bob started shaking badly and Philip moved in to support him.

When Bob got steady, he ran to his son. Jake had already carried to body out of the brush, and it looked like Billy was sleeping. When Bob reached him he fell down next to the boy and was on the ground hugging his son and crying. Philip and Jake stayed back and let Bob grieve. He was sobbing loudly, and after awhile, the sobbing subdued. He lay there with his boy for what seemed to be a very long time. He had been stroking the boy's hair. Finally, Bob kissed his son on the forehead and stood up. He had control again, and asked Jake, "What happened to him?"

Jake quietly spoke and said, "I think Billy was down here either to water the horses, or maybe he was following some game. There were several prints of horses with no shoes, and two horses that were shod. I assumed that a Comanche raiding party spotted him without him seeing them. They probably hid and set up an ambush for him. When he was close enough, they let go their arrows."

Philip said, "We had heard that the Indians were stealing horses in the area. We have never had any trouble with them, or even seen any around here before."

Jake said, "They shot him with arrows and most likely took the horses, your rifle, and Philip's knife. Bob, I think that shot we heard earlier today was Billy getting off a round when he realized what was happening."

Jake said, "Bob come with me, I want to show you something." The three men walked past Billy for several more feet. Jake said, "Look, there is lots of blood on these rocks here," as he pointed down. "I think Billy was surprised by the ambush but had the where-with-all to get a shot off, and he hit one of the raiders. He either killed or wounded him. Either way, his brothers put him on a horse and left with him. If he was wounded, with all that blood lost, I'm pretty sure he died then, or soon thereafter. Billy was a very brave man."

Without talking, the men picked up Billy and carried the body all the way back up to where the horses were tied. They carefully draped Billy over the spare horse, and gently tied him to the saddle. Nobody spoke during the ride back either. The horses moved at a snail pace so that Billy would stay secure. When they got back to the ranch, they gently removed the body and laid him down on a soft patch of hay in the barn. By that time, it was late afternoon.

Bob looked at the brothers with very sad eyes. He said, "Listen Philip and Jake, I do not blame you in any way for this. You simply helped a young man who wanted to show his father that he was a man. I will always grieve for my son, but I will never blame either of you for this. I gave him permission to go, and I too had heard tales of rogue Indians in this part of Texas. It was simply a terrible tragedy."

Jake said, "I will build a coffin tonight, and tomorrow we will give him a Christian burial."

Bob nodded and said, "I will fetch Lottie and Abigail, and I will bring them here so they can show their love to the son and brother. When we are through, we will retire, although, we most likely will spend the night with Billy here." Philip went and got a lantern which was full of oil, and he gave it to Bob along with a box of matches.

Philip told Bob, "This lantern should have enough oil to burn all night. If it gets low, there is a full jar of oil over there," and he pointed. Jake and Philip both hugged Bob and each was crying. Philip asked Bob, "Bob, would you like for one of us to stay with you?"

Jake said, "Bob, I will tell Lottie and Abigail that they need to go to the barn."

When he entered the house, Jake quietly told Caroline what had happened. Jake then walked over to Billy's sister and mom. He told them with a very serious, voice, "Bob would like you to go out to the barn."

Lottie asked Jake, "Is something wrong?"

Jake told her in a very soft voice, "You need to go to the barn." Lottie and Abigail left the house quickly and were very nervous. When they got to the barn, Bob was standing outside, and he told them what had happened as he was hugged by his beloved girls. The Smith house was very quiet and sad. There wasn't the usual banter and laughter. Everyone was stricken with the grief of Billy's death. Philip spoke, "Tomorrow morning, I will find an appropriate place to bury the young man. We will dig the grave and I will give a sermon, since there is no man of the cloth nearby us."

Jake said, "I will make a coffin and a cross. If it doesn't bother the family, I will ask them if I can do my work in the barn."

Chapter 56
The Smith Cemetery at School Creek

The next day began early for them all. Jake had been working almost all night to construct a decent coffin, and form a wooden cross that looked very respectful. In the early morning, Philip walked 300 steps from his house directly north, and put a stake under a live oak tree.(1) "This will be where Billy Walker will rest in peace," he said out loud, with no one to hear, except himself.

Philip, Jake, Bob, and the ranch hands took turns at digging the grave. When they finished, Philip said, "How do you want to do this Bob?"

Bob told him, "Let's go back and get cleaned up and we can all gather at Billy's grave."

Philip said, "That sounds like a good idea. I think Caroline and Lottie are cooking so that we can have a hot meal after the ceremony. I will give the sermon, if it's okay with you, Bob. Bob nodded and they all walked back to the house, without speaking.

After everybody cleaned up, they put on their best clothes. They met in the Smith's living room, all held hands, and Jake said a beautiful prayer. Caroline and Lottie had prepared the body for his burial. When it was time, Bob, Philip, Jake and Antonio lifted Billy and placed him in his coffin. They nailed the top down well. The men picked up the covered coffin with reverence, and put it into the back of the wagon. Bob asked, "May I drive the wagon to his gravesite?

Philip said "Of course Bob." He drove the wagon slowly and everyone else walked behind the wagon as one.

The same four men gently lifted the coffin from the wagon. With the help of ropes under the coffin, the men carefully lowered Billy into his grave. Everyone gathered around the young man's grave. Philip provided a very respectful and moving ceremony. The ranch hands had filled in the grave after the others left. Bob, Philip and Jake stayed behind. Bob said, "I would like to set the cross for my son." No one spoke, yet everyone bowed their head in agreement.

Jake handed the handmade cross to Bob, and walked with him to where the cross would be set. Jake carried a large hammer, similar to a sledge hammer. Jake handed the hammer to Bob, and held the cross in place as Bob pounded the cross until it was solidly set into the ground. Philip said one more prayer for Billy with everyone standing around the new grave. Then they walked together quietly and with great respect, back to the house.

The ladies had warmed up the lunch while others sat and talked quietly. Jake said, "It was a beautiful ceremony for a beautiful young man."

Philip spoke up and told Bob, "I am so sorry about your loss, and I want to tell you that your beautiful family can stay on the Smith Ranch for as long as you want. You can even build a house on the ranch and be a ranch hand if you choose."

Bob looked Philip square in the eyes and said, "Thank you my friend. Lottie and I talked a long time last night. We came to the conclusion that we needed to continue on our adventure, and keep going on to California. We will be leaving tomorrow morning. I am sad that I will be so far away from my son, and may never be able to visit his grave. All I know is that he is with people who love him, and I know that you will visit him, and care for his grave."

"I ask for just one thing, please tell him that his father loves him with all his heart. And also tell him that his dad told you that he was a kind, brave man, and I couldn't be any prouder of him."

Philip replied, "I will visit him often, and I will tend to him for the rest of my life. And know this, if you and Lottie ever even get close to this place, promise me you will visit."

Bob nodded slowly and said, "Thank you."

The next morning, the Walkers were packed, and the wagon was loaded, and they were ready to go. The Smiths and the ranch hands came outside to say their good-byes. After some hugs, crying, and a scattering of quiet chatter, the Bob Walker family drove off to their destiny.

Philip felt joy and knew that they would be all right. Bob turned around on the bench, saw Philip and Jake, then smiled and waved for a long time. The Smith brothers waved back, themselves smiling. Then, in a few minutes, the brothers lost sight of the wagon. The brothers turned and went into the house.

After talking to Caroline and Jake the next day, Philip announced, "I will go to Burleson, and find a surveyor to come survey a piece of land to include Billy's grave. I will donate the land to be a community cemetery." The next morning he saddled up and went to town and talked to a surveyor who told him that he would come out as soon as possible. Billy Walker was the first human being to be buried in the "Smith Cemetery at School Creek."

The surveyor came out a few days later to survey the plot of land that would be the cemetery. He left a copy of the survey with Philip and told him to register the deed with the county. Philip had donated one half of an acre for the cemetery. Burleson had an assistant clerk who could register and file the deed. Philip thanked the surveyor, and gave him payment for his services.

The current Smith Cemetery at School Creek
Lampasas County, Texas (2019)

The tree line in the distance defines the border of the Lampasas River

Chapter 57
And Life Goes On

After the Walkers left, everything had gotten back to normal. Philip was always working on his house when he wasn't doing ranch work. It was coming along very well. Philip and Caroline had invited Jake to stay in the big house, and he accepted and was very happy. His little log cabin wasn't much and he was quite social. He loved being around his brother and his family. The year had become 1855.

The next day, Caroline had come across the fabric that she and Julia had picked out in LaGrange. She called for Julia to come to her. Julia came running and asked her mom, "What is it mother?"

Caroline had the fabric behind her and asked the child, "Do you want to learn to sew?"

Julia grinned as Caroline brought the fabric from behind her back. The girl could hardly contain herself and said, "I love you mom, I am so excited." Caroline and Julia sat down. Caroline had Julia use hand over hand to make her dress. By the time they finished with Julia's dress, Caroline let her, with a little help, make the dress for Dolly to match her own.

At the dinner table one evening, Jake told Philip, "There is talk in town that the state legislature is going to redraw the county lines. That will make our ranch a part of a new county, Lampasas County." By election, the Texas legislature did exactly that. On March 10, 1856, Lampasas County was created. The law also ruled that the County Seat would be the town with the same name as the new county. The town of Burleson officially became the town of Lampasas. (1)

Jake worked with his brother on the house, and everything was going well. Philip had a delivery of several cut blocks of native limestone. The men who had delivered the stones, with help from his brother and the ranch hands, unloaded the stones right next to the house. Philip had measured, and figured the exact number of stones he would need as well as where each stone would be.

He also had a custom book shelf cut that would be a part of the living room wall. The cedar beams were still in the barn, and would be placed after the walls were set and mortared. After the stones were set, he would raise the beams and built a sturdy roof. He also had figured where the fireplace would stand as a part of the wall, which was also in the living room.

The brothers were very good ranchers and it was paying off, and they loved it. On a bright warm early September day, the cowboys were rounding up some stray steers near the river. Jake saw something up by the main road. He told Philip, "Hey brother, there is a wagon turning in to our road."

Philip looked and replied, "Sure enough, we have company." The wagon was covered and had two people on the bench and two horses tied to the back of the wagon. The brothers started herding the strays back to the corrals with a couple of ranch hands. Jake told the hands, "You guys take it from here." They did, and the two brothers kicked their steeds and galloped toward the visitors. When they got close enough to recognize the people, Philip shouted, "I can't believe what I see, that is Pedro and his wife, Felicia." It had been almost 2 years since they last saw Pedro. Both Smith boys were amazed at the sight.

The two men reached the wagon before the wagon was able to make it to the house. Philip and Jake came to a roaring halt at the wagon, and at the same time, hopped off their horses. Pedro had come to a stop also. He jumped down off the wagon and said, "Hi Philip and Jake, I speak some English now." The men hugged their friend and were full of joy. Pedro said in broken English, "This is my wife, Felicia."

Philip and Jake both tipped their hats and Jake said, "So nice to finally meet you Felicia, all Pedro could do when we were traveling is to talk about you guys and the ranch."

Jake told Pedro. "We have a place for you to live and we are so glad you came back."

Philip said, "As of this moment, you will be the ranch manager of the Smith Ranch. Let's go surprise Caroline, and especially Julia. Albert is two years old now."

The brothers rode ahead of the wagon and stopped and hopped off the horses. They went into the house. Jake yelled, "Everybody come out front, we've got visitors." They all came out and Julia spotted Pedro right away. She ran straight to him and jumped up as Pedro caught her with a big hug. Julia was crying happy tears and saying, "Oh Pedro, I thought I would never see you again. I am so happy."

Pedro told her while pointing, "This is my wife, Felicia, and she has wanted to meet you as soon as I got home. I couldn't stop talking to her about you." Jake helped Felicia down off the wagon. Julia ran to her and hugged her as if she had known Felicia for her entire life.

The couple came into the house and they felt very welcome. Philip told them, "We have a small cabin down by the river where Jake had been living. He moved in with us, and from now on the house is yours." We will show you where it is and you can drive the wagon down to the cabin. But tonight, you are our guests. We can help you move in tomorrow." Pedro and Felicia were filled with happiness. They ate dinner in the big house and Caroline and Julia had created a makeshift bed on the floor in the living room for the couple to sleep on that night.

The couple moved into the cabin the next day. Pedro became the ranch manager and he had a great deal of experience with cattle. He also had a great instinct to be a leader of the ranch hands. It was all good at the ranch. Felicia was a natural with Julia and Albert. She would tend to the children whenever Caroline worked on her farming, gardening or was otherwise busy. Felicia was also a good cook and she helped with meals quite a bit. The children adopted her as their grandmother right away. Things were at peace.

It was in the year of 1856 that Caroline gave birth to her third healthy child, a boy named William J. Smith. He would always be known as Will. He was my great grandfather.

Chapter 58
Troublemaker, Scene II

After breakfast one day, Jake spoke up and said, "Well folks, I have a surprise for you all. When you finish here, I would like all of you to come down to the pens. Please wait about 10 minutes or so to come down." Everyone was extremely curious about what Jake was up to. He left the house without speaking and went down to the pens. Philip and the others had built some holding pens for the new cattle as well as the other animals such as the sheep, goats, and a few pigs.

As Jake was eating breakfast with the family, Pedro and the other hands had found Troublemaker and separated him from the herd. They drove him to one of the pens where there was a ranch hand standing, and a cowboy was holding the gate open. The wranglers drove Troublemaker into the pen as the ranch hand shut the gate behind him.

The bull had matured and was the biggest and strongest bull in the herd. He was a beautiful, powerful animal. One could sense the power of that bull simply by gazing at him. Pedro tossed a lasso over the animal's head and pulled the rope tight. A couple of ranch hands had also looped ropes around the bull's neck. By that time, Jake had made it down to the pen.

The small crowd had walked down to the pen and most of them were pretty sure that they knew what was about to happen. Jake slipped through the gate as a ranch hand quickly opened a small gap for him to go through. The people around him were hollering and giving Jake a very hard time. Jake shouted to the audience, "Well, if any of you remember crossing the Colorado River, I guess you know what comes next. I promised I would ride this bull someday, and today is the day. I will ride this monster for at least 8 seconds, as I said."

Pedro and the ranch hands were trying to keep the bull steady, but he was not cooperating. It was all they could do to try. Jake yelled at the top of his lungs saying, "I'm going to ride this bull!" Another ranch hand was standing right beside Troublemaker. The cowboy had squatted down and had his hands cupped. Jake started running towards the animal.

Jake leaped into the cowboys entwined fingers of both hands. Jake gracefully landed on the man's cupped hands with one foot. At the same time the cowboy vaulted him into the air. Jake landed on to the back of the bull. Simultaneously, Pedro and the other guys let go of the ropes right when Jake landed on the bull's back. Within 2 seconds, the bull bucked and launched Jake into the air at the moment of contact. Troublemaker bucked so hard it caused Jake to fly about 10 feet away from the bull. Jake landed with a thud squarely on his back.

The onlookers were thunderstruck while Jake laid there motionless. The folks were scared that Jake was hurt badly or possibly was dead. Then Philip hollered, "Jake, are you okay?" Jake stayed still for a long pause without moving. He then hopped to his feet and screamed, "Yahoo!", as he threw his arms straight up into the air. Jake hobbled from the pen with a giant smile on his face. Philip shouted, "Jake's got a hitch in his gitty up!" Everyone scurried to Jake and the guys patted him on the back and the ladies (including Julia) kissed him on the cheek.

After that wonderful moment, time began to pass with the mundane ranch work, and things were about the same. The brothers and Pedro continued to work a successful cattle ranch with the children and the ranch hands. Philip finished building his house in late 1856. It turned out to be a wonderful home.

Lightning lived a long life, but he was showing his age after many years. Philip wouldn't let anyone ride him again. Philip would go see him every evening and put a halter on him. The two would walk to the best place to graze that was nearest to the barn. And every day when they were through, Philip would always have a treat, usually a carrot. It was Lightning's favorite treat. Philip walked his best friend until the day that Lightning passed away.

Philip's house is standing in the exact spot where it was built. The Smith's lived in it for many years and eventually sold it with some land. The house has been modernized, yet, it looks a great deal like the original house.

Philip and Caroline's House
The home is currently owned and lived in by Robert and Alicia Straley

The house had been remodeled and modernized since 1856. This is the current condition. Philip and Caroline did not have a satellite dish.

The original fireplace built into the limestone blocks.

The original cedar beams that Philip, Jake and friends set. If you look at the window on the left, you can see the window that was set in the two foot wall.

The custom bookcase that was set into the wall.

These photos are of Philip's original house which was finished in 1856. He continued to work on it for a few more years. Robert and Alicia Straley currently own and live in the home. They were gracious to allow us to go into the house and take photographs. The house has been modernized through the many years. It has changed ownership a few times. I took these photographs in 2019. The State of Texas awarded an historical marker for the house in 1966.

Chapter 59

Jacob Smith, II, Better Known as "Jake," Shows His Heart

Jake had never gotten married. Honestly, there were very few candidates in such an unpopulated territory. He went to a few dances in Lampasas, but they were few and far between. He was a Christian, and people would gather at a different ranch each Sunday and he would attend service. There was a traveling pastor that came sometimes, but usually it was a rancher or ranch hand that performed the service. Jake gave the service many times. Philip, Caroline and the children almost always attended the services.

The years passsed by with peace and harmony prevailing. After several years had passed, the family received a letter from Elizabeth. In the letter, she told them, *"Dear ones, your father got sick and he passed away in his sleep. We buried him next to Henry Philip in our family cemetery. I am sad and yet realize that death comes to all. I loved him and will miss him. Please try to send me a letter to let me know how you folks are. I am doing well for an old lady. All my love, Mom"*

One night after dinner in late autumn, Jake and Philip were sitting on the front porch talking. Jake told Philip, "Brother, you and Caroline have been so good to me through these years." Philip kind of twisted his face some and was wondering why his brother was speaking this way.

He told Jake, "Jacob, I don't know what our life would be like without you. I don't think we could have done anything without you being there every step of the way." He rarely spoke his brother's given name.

Jake's chin was on his chest and he said, "I am going to donate some of my land so that the folks can have a place to build a real church. And, I have decided that after that, I will give you and Caroline the remainder of my land. I then will be going home to Matagorda."

Philip was very moved by what his brother had just told him. He scrambled to think of what to say to him. There was a long pause, and he spoke and said, "Jake, I really don't have any words to tell you except that I love and respect you more than any one on earth, except for maybe Caroline." They both sat on the porch for a very long time before they spoke. Philip finally told him, "Jake, you are such a joy to be around and often you play the clown, but I know you to be the most decent, intelligent person that I have ever known. I'm sure you have thought this plan over completely. You know I will always support you with anything you do."

They got up and went into the house to prepare for bed. Before they went inside, Philip grabbed Jake and pulled him to his chest. As he was giving Jake a bear hug he whispered in his ear, "I'll miss you so much." Without another word, the two went to their rooms.

Jake told Philip the next day, "I am riding to Lampasas tomorrow and will probably spend the night there. I have some business to take care of. Philip nodded to his brother and knew exactly what he was going to do. The next morning, Jake saddled up and headed out to town. While he was there, he deeded two acres to build the School Creek Baptist Church.

He enjoyed a little poker and some beer that night in the saloon. A touch of irony, I suppose. He went back to the ranch. Jake wrote a note, *'I am happy to be able to give the elders a deed of land for the School Creek Baptist Church.'*(3) Jake gave Philip the deed and the note and asked him "Please give them to the elders". Philip nodded, and took the note.

Jake stayed about a week with his family. There was a break, and Jake looked into Philip's eyes and said, "You know

Philip, for the last few months I have thought about mom and dad, and our brothers and sisters. Mom is getting old."

Jacob, Sr. and Elizabeth had eleven children. Their son, John, was killed in the Battle of Atlanta during the Civil War. Six of their children had married, and left for a variety of places including Philip, Jake, and Emily who had married Caroline's brother John Russler.

On a day, much like others, Jake packed his bags to leave. Philip had agreed early on that they co-owned everything on the ranch, so he told Jake to take any animal or thing he wanted with him. He packed one horse, and had one horse to ride. He was standing out front when he gave a loud whistle. He had *Little Troublemaker* tied behind the pack horse. *Little Troublemaker* was an offspring of *Troublemaker I,* and he was two years old. He was the spitting image of *Troublemaker I.*

The other Smiths came out from the house. Philip had provided Jake with several gold coins from the savings account and said, "You know what we went through before, guard your money and be very careful along the way." Jake hugged each of his family members and held each one for a long time. Jake said to Philip, "A wagon would just slow us down, and we can all swim the Colorado River pretty easily".

Jake continued, "I'm not going to let this be mushy, so just remember me with good thoughts. I love you all and always will, and now I'm leaving. Please don't say anything, just try to smile as I go."

Philip said, "I'm going to break the rule. I have two things I want you to do when you get home. First, give a hug to mom for me, and the other is to please write us a letter that you had reached home safely. You know our mailing address. Good luck and watch your surroundings."

Jake smiled and said, "Philip, you just can't be silent can you? I love you brother and all of you folks too. Now I'm gone." Jake tied the extra horse to his saddle horn. He secured *Little Troublemaker* to the pack horse. He mounted his horse. He wanted to go fast but he could only go as fast as the bull calf could walk. He didn't ever turn his head back, because he knew he couldn't have handled it. He had tears rolling down his cheeks as he rode away. Everyone at the house stood still as they watched their beloved Jake until he went out of sight.

They returned to the house. Philip advised his family, "We will all miss Jake. He was a bright light that had led us for many years. Only think of him in the best way. He taught all of us so much."

Philip had sent a letter to their mom telling her that everyone was well, and Jake is on his way back to Matagorda.

The family remained working the ranch, going to church and having more cows, chickens, pigs, horses, tears, laughter and hugs. Philip and Caroline had eight children in Lampasas County. They also had Henry Philip who died in infancy and Julia who was born in Matagorda. Albert was born on the **Arduous Journey**.

The original School Creek Baptist Church

The church was built and completed on April 27, 1901 on the land that Jacob Smith, Jr. donated for that specific purpose. The church building was active for many years, and the congregation grew too large to hold all the church goers. The church members built a larger building on the land in 2004 in able to receive the many folks that choose to worship there.

Chapter 60
Lampasas Joins the Gilded Age

"The period in the U.S. circa, 1870-98 was characterized by a greatly expanding economy, known as the Gilded Age." (13) The town of Lampasas was part of that Gilded Age. The town had seven springs in and around the town. Several had a great deal of minerals in their waters.

Around 1880, a group of wealthy men from Galveston had discovered the small town and the springs. These men decided that they could make this town a destination for tourists, like Hot Springs and Saratoga.

A few wealthy business men began to build hotels and bath houses that had heated mineral water baths. The largest hotel was the Park Hotel which was a little more than a mile from the railroad depot. More hotels and mineral baths were built near the other springs around the area.

1883 was the beginning of an eruption of commerce in Lampasas, Texas. It lasted until the early 1890's. The entrepreneurs started advertising in Dallas, San Antonio, Houston, and Galveston for tourists to visit the hot mineral baths. People began to come to this new tourist town. The informal name for Lampasas became, "The Saratoga of the South." Visitors from the big cities would take the train from their home town and get off at the depot in Lampasas.

The wealthy owners got together and built tracks from the depot to the Park Hotel. The Keystone Hotel was a one block walk from the train depot. The visitors would ride on a mule-drawn trolley car on tracks from the train depot to other destinations. The tourists took the trolley back when they were leaving town. The Park Hotel was built of wood and glass in 1883 and had 200 rooms. It sadly burned to the ground in February, 1895. (14) This was the beginning of the end of major tourism in Lampasas. At the peak of the tourism, Lampasas had a population of approximately 20,000.(6)

Today it has a population under 10,000 people, yet is a thriving community. During the era of that time, there were opera houses, boating, roller skating and of course, the wonderful curative baths.(15)

The historic Hostess House

HISTORIC
HOSTESS HOUSE
at
HANCOCK SPRINGS

The historic Hancock Springs

The free flowing swimming pool fed by Hancock Springs

Texas state historical marker near Hancock Springs

The historic Keystone Hotel in Lampasas. The structure was built as a stagecoach inn during the 1860's, and 10 rooms were added on in the 1870's. It continued to expand. The hotel is a block from the train depot and was very busy during the Gilded Age and far beyond.(16) Andrew Fish from Austin, and Debbie Reynolds have renovated the run down hotel back to her glory days.

From left to right, Dr. Lloyd S. Smith, Roger Carpenter and, we believe that
the last fellow is a chauffeur who is waiting on big wigs inside the
Keystone Hotel, circa, 1934. Lloyd is my father and Roger is my second
cousin. Roger was mayor of Lampasas for several terms.

The Lampasas County Courthouse.
The courthouse was built in 1883-84. It is one of the 5 oldest Texas
courthouses still in use today. There are 254 counties in the state of Texas.
(18)

Smith Family Historical Footnotes

Will J. Smith

Will J. Smith was the second white child born in Lampasas County, and the first child born of Philip and Caroline in Lampasas County. He was my great grandfather. The first born child was Cornelius McAnelly, who was born on the western side of the county near the Colorado River. He was born a couple of months before Will. I have luckily become the owner of Will's felt Stetson cowboy hat that he wore every day on the ranch. It has a few nibbles by worms and other signs of age, but it is in excellent shape and fits on my head swimmingly. He must have had large ears because the hat shows wear on the bottom of the brim where his ears would be when he pulled the hat down tightly. And that was probably most of the time.(1)

Will Smith and Cornelius McAnelly (L-R) were both 90 years old for this photograph. Mr. McAnelly was the first white child born in Lampasas County, Texas. Mr. Smith was the second born two months later, in 1856.

Will grew up on the ranch, and when he was in his 20's, he married Mary Stanley. They had two boys, Philip and William Walter. Walter, as he was called, was my grandfather. Will and Mary were living in Philip and Caroline's house.

My grandfather wrote two historical essays regarding the Philip Smith story. In one, he told the story that Will had found a nice, small wooden house in Lampasas that was for sale for cheap. He asked his father if he could buy the house and move it to the ranch. Philip agreed, yet Walter never detailed how the house moving was completed.

After doing research, the most common ways to move a house back then were, *(a)* Take every board down, number each board, move the pieces and rebuild the house using the numbering system. *(b)* At that time period, some buildings were moved by creating wooden rails that were greased. One horse would circle a **capstan**, which is similar to the machine that raises an anchor for ships. The horse would rotate around the capstan and it would pull the building by tightening the attached chains.(15) This process was primarily used in towns and cities for short distances. *(c)* I think this is what Philip and Will did. They would take the railings off of two wagons, and then extend the surface of the wagons by attaching boards to connect the two wagons. Then they would raise the house with jacks, pulleys and lots of manpower. With any of these processes, it would have been an ordeal. I do know that the house was moved from the City of Lampasas to the Smith Ranch.

Philip deeded land to Will where the new house was. Will and Mary lived in the house for the rest of their lives. Walter, one of Will and Mary's children grew up in the house and when he was an adult, he inherited it. He was my grandfather.

(L-R) **Will**, **Philip III**, **Mary**, *and* **Walter Smith** *at their new home, circa 1885 Walter would eventually inherit this home. Walter married Alta Carpenter, and they had only one child, a boy named Lloyd Sidney Smith. That was my father, and he was the last Smith child born on the ranch. He was born in this house.*

The Story Continues

The story of Jacob and Elizabeth Smith began in 1833 when they left their home in Germany and settled in Matagorda, Texas. As a reminder, Jacob and Elizabeth were the parents of Philip and Jake. As of 2019, there have been eight generations of the Smith family in Texas. The story continued when Philip, Caroline, Jacob, Jr., and Julia left the Texas coast, and doggedly pursued becoming settlers themselves. Through trials and tribulations, they settled in the uninhabited area of rural Lampasas County, Texas. The Smith family and other brave families were the forefathers and foremothers of this part of the world. I am proud to be a descendent of these good and hard working people.

Philip died on May 17, 1907, and there is no evidence that he was ever attended by a doctor in his life. Caroline died on January 6, 1880, having had a long marriage, and the birth of 11 children.

This ends a chapter of an amazing American family of which I am very proud. As far as I can tell, they all were decent, honest, happy, hard working folks that also were humble and they lived honorably.

PHILIP SMITH
BORN
DEC 22 1821
DIED
MAY 17 1907

In my father's house
are many mansions.
CAROLINE L.
WIFE OF
PHILIP SMITH
BORN
OCT. 27, 1826
DIED
JAN. 26, 1880

Comments

When a person faces fear and trepidation, some persevere, and they are the brave. This story is the real history of Jacob, Elizabeth, Philip, Caroline and Jake Smith. They were German immigrants who survived almost unbeatable odds to reach their goals. Somehow they overcame many hardships as they took on a courageous undertaking to reach their dreams. They made a mark, not only for themselves, but for a small, yet important, mark on the great history of Texas and America. I am not sure that I could survive the struggles that they had to endure.

My grandfather, Walter, was the first of the family to graduate from high school. He loved the ranch, but times were changing and he mostly leased the land to other cattle owners. He still had a small herd but he worked as a traveling school teacher primarily in northern Lampasas County. He and his wife and child eventually moved into town. Walter worked in Lampasas for the Post Office, and he eventually became the Assistant Postmaster. He kept the ranch and would spend time there often.

My father, Lloyd Sidney Smith, was the last Smith child born on the ranch. The success of the ranch had been formed through hard work, grit and love. There were also great and happy times. My dad was an only child, and he reminds me so much of Philip. Both men had a passion to learn and the courage needed to succeed. From a Central Texas ranch, my dad envisioned so much more.

After he graduated from high school in Lampasas, Texas, he attended Howard Payne College. He had married his sweetheart, Margaret (Wooten) Smith and she worked to pay the cost of living, and kept them going while dad continued his education. Mom graduated as the Salutatorian of her class at Lampasas High School. Mom raised four boys who all became good men. She was a pioneer woman at heart and spirit, and she could have thrived in the time of Philip and Caroline. After college, dad was accepted into The University of Texas Dental School in Houston, Texas.

Dad excelled in school, and graduated with a DDS degree. He joined what was then the Army Air Corps. Soon after that, the corps morphed into the U.S. Air Force. He entered service as a first lieutenant and retired after 28 years of service as a Full (or Bird) Colonel. Prior to his military service, he had worked as the dentist for the CCC camp south of Burnet, Texas. Many men worked hard to build structures and make Longhorn Cavern viable for the public to visit. It is now part of Inks Lake State Park. Dad also served in World War II in China, and in South Korea during the Korean Conflict.

This is a photograph of my father, Dr. Lloyd S. Smith, in China during World War II. He is holding a shield that was the logo of the Flying Tigers Squadron. The pilots and crew were all volunteers from the U.S. Air Force and were stationed there from 1941 to 1942. The Japanese Air Force and Navy had blocked most of the ports in China and other strategic places of the allies. The Flying Tigers fearlessly fought the Japanese planes over The Burma and China Seas and helped to clear the ports.(6)

Post Script

Seven generations of Smiths have enjoyed and worked on the Smith Ranch. The Smith Cemetery at School Creek began when a 15 year old pioneer traveling with his family was buried there by Philip Smith. The cemetery is not a family cemetery, it was always meant to be a community cemetery. It is a thriving cemetery in a rural area that has people from many places laid to rest there.

The current people buried there were 343 as of late 2018. The cemetery holds many veterans, including the Texas Revolutionary War, the Civil War, WWI, WWII, the Korean Conflict, the Vietnam Conflict, and the Middle East Conflicts. Most of my relatives are resting where Philip, Caroline, and Jake cultivated a cattle ranch which still looks very much like it did in the 1850's. Most of my relatives, other than the ones that stayed or returned to Matagorda, are buried in this cemetery.

I also wanted to tell you that the School Creek Baptist Church is thriving, and it has many people in the congregation. An amount of thanks goes to Jake for his help, but mostly thanks to the wonderful people who have made the church what it is today.

Philip received a letter from Jake two months from when he left the Lampasas Smith Ranch. The letter stated: *"Dear Family, I made it back to Matagorda! The trip was fine and the roads have gotten much better. Mom passed away recently and she arranged for me to run the ranch. I will never forget our journey and starting a new cattle ranch. I hope you are all well and I love each and every one of you. Don't forget to smile brother. All my love, Jake."*

This Story Tells Itself

I need to tell one more story that really moved me. I was doing research for a state historical cemetery marker for the Smith Cemetery at School Creek where I read each head stone.

I read the head stone of Owen B. Butts. I saw this headstone and it caught my eye. This stone moved me greatly when I realized the story that it told.

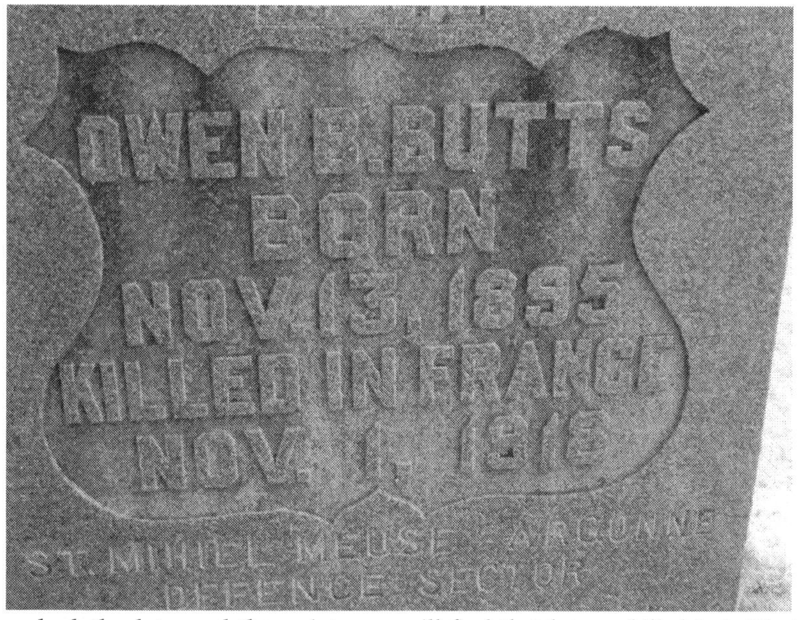

If you check the dates and the script, you will find that he was killed in battle in France 10 days before World War I ended, and 12 days before he would have turned 23 years old.

It struck me so strongly that a young man with the majority of his life ahead of him, had died serving his country and the world when he was 22 years old. He would have been coming home in 10 days, and would have had his 23rd birthday in 12 days if he hadn't been killed in action in France. America truly has been primarily built by brave immigrants looking to make a better life for themselves and their family.

The thoughts reinforced my philosophy that we should never take one day on earth for granted. If anyone in your family has not recorded your family's history, please consider writing or audio recording your family history. You will be glad you did. I have been. Thanks to my grandfather and father, who both wrote down as much history as they knew about the families of Jacob Smith, Sr., and that of Philip Smith. That spurred me to write this book. I hope that you enjoyed the story of the Philip Smith family. Jake indeed ran the ranch which had become much smaller. Elizabeth had divided the big ranch and gave a parcel of land to each child and also sold some land. Jake met a wonderful lady and fell in love. He did get married after all. He led a happy life and lived to be 87 years old. I am very lucky to have come from this family. And remember, every family has a story to tell.

The Historical Marker designated on the exact house and location where Philip and his family lived in 1854 and beyond. Jake lived in the home for a long time until he decided to return to Matagorda to run the first Smith Ranch. Robert and Alicia Straley now live in this beautiful, historical home.

References

1. **William Walter Smith**: Grandson of Philip Smith. He provided written and oral history of the Jacob Smith family, with a focus on Philip Smith. Philip was my paternal grandfather.

2. **Lloyd S. Smith**: Great grandson of Philip Smith. He provided written and oral history of the Smith family history also. He was my father.

3. **Henry Langford**, rancher. Provided oral and written history of Jacob Smith, Jr., Philip Smith and School Creek Baptist Church. Henry has served as the steward of the Smith Cemetery at School Creek for the past few decades.

4. **Lampasas County Texas, "It's history and It's people,"** Lampasas County Historical commission. Walswort Publishing Co., Marceline, MO, 1991.

5. **LampasasCountyCemeteries,1856-1995,**Lampasas Historical Commission. Eakin Press, Austin, TX, 1995

6. www.wikipedia.org./ online encyclopedia.

7. **www.history.com/** online resource

8. **www.americanhistory.si.edu/** online resource

9. **www.reference.com/**online resource

10. **Article, "*Who was who in Lampasas, County,*"** published in the **Lampasas Record Newspaper**, on April 25, 1959. Written by E.M. Pharr.

11. **NBC Television Network**, game show, "*Who wants to be a Millionaire.*"Question, "What Greek words were the origin of the modern day name, 'Philip' or 'Phillip'?"

12. **Webster's Unabridged Dictionary, 2ndedition.** Random House Reference

13. **www.TrulyTexas.com,** online reference.

14. **<u>Images of America, Lampasas County</u>**. Lampasas County Museum Foundation, Inc. 2009. Published by Arcadia Publishing.

15. **<u>https://gtjournal.tadl.org/2014/when-horsepower-was-literal-moving-in-the-1890s</u>**. **<u>Grand TraveseJournal</u>**: Amy Barrit, September 1, 2014, online resource

16. **KWTX** television station, Waco, Texas

17. **<u>Matagorda County, Texas. Marriage Records, 1837-1899</u>**. Matagorda County Genealogical Society, Bay City, Texas

18. **<u>Postcard History Series, Lampasas County</u>**. Lampasas Museum Foundation, Inc., Published by *Arcadia Publishing*, Charleston, South Carolina.

About the Author

Greg with his wife, Melissa, in the northern Cascade Range of Washington State, with Mt. Baker in the background.

Lloyd Gregory Smith was born in Austin, Texas in 1949. He graduated from McCallum High School in Austin, and attended The University of Texas – Austin, then transferred to Southwest Texas State University. He graduated with a B.S. in Biology, with minors in Chemistry and Anthropology. He had the calling to teach, which had been with him since he was a child. He went on to receive a M.Ed. in Counseling and Guidance, with honors. He also has lifetime teaching certificates in Secondary Composite Science. He is qualified to teach every secondary science course offered in Texas Public Schools (grades 6 through 12).

Better known as "Greg," he taught 7 years of middle school earth science, and served at all levels as a school counselor for 32 more years. After high school, he entered college as an

English major with a desire to be a writer. He got a little sidetracked when he fell in love with science. After retirement from education, he finally took the step and wrote this book.

Greg is married to his sweetheart, Melissa, and has been for more than 45 years. The couple has two grown children, Kristin Smith who lives in Bellingham, Washington, and Steven Smith and his wife, Shannah, who live in Honolulu, Hawaii. Greg's true, endearing loves are God and family. Closely behind are his love of true friends, dogs, science (especially geology), traveling, wildlife, pristine scenery, sports, and music.

I wish everyone a happy and fulfilling life. ☺

Made in the USA
Lexington, KY
07 December 2019